Essential Cognitive Therapy

Essential Cognitive Therapy

MICHAEL NEENAN

Centre for Stress Management, London

AND

WINDY DRYDEN

Goldsmiths College, University of London

W

WHURR PUBLISHERS

LONDON AND PHILADELPHIA

©2000 Whurr Publishers Ltd
First published 2000 by
Whurr Publishers Ltd
19b Compton Terrace, London N1 2UN, England

Reprinted 2001, 2002, 2004 and 2005

British Library Cataloguing in Publication Data
A catalogue record for this book is available from
the British Library.

ISBN: 186156 173 3

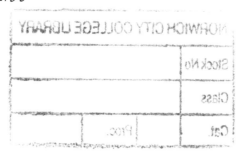
Printed and bound by CPI Antony Rowe, Eastbourne

Contents

Preface

Cognitive therapy (CT) is being applied to an ever increasing number of clinical problems and populations (Dattilio and Freeman, 1992; Salkovskis, 1996; Clark and Fairburn, 1997). Beck (1995) suggests that CT can be used with non-psychiatric populations such as prison inmates and schoolchildren, while Richman (1992) shows how to apply it in the workplace. Additions to cognitive theory provide further clarification and refinement (Clark, 1995; Beck, 1996; Wells, 1997). In fact, as Salkovskis (1996, p. 539) points out, 'the rate of development of cognitive theory and therapy has been unprecedented'. Although this 'rate of development' has produced a vast literature, newcomers to CT (students and experienced therapists alike) can feel overwhelmed by this literature and wonder which book to read that will explain CT in a straightforward way?

This book was written with this question in mind and is organized into six chapters. Chapter 1 describes key elements of CT theory and practice. The main section of the book, Chapters 2–5, shows CT in action as we follow the progress of our client, Paul (not his real name), from assessment to termination. We have included dialogue excerpts from therapy in order to demonstrate the techniques and procedures we have described. The last chapter examines some of the usual difficulties experienced by clients and counsellors in therapy (though, of course, these difficulties are not exclusive to CT). We hope that we have written the book in an easy-to-read style but the use of some CT jargon was unavoidable (this jargon can always be translated into client-friendly terms as we show).

Chapter One
An Outline of Cognitive Therapy

In this chapter we discuss key aspects of cognitive therapy (CT) theory and practice, including understanding clients' constructions of their realities, presenting an information-processing model of psychological functioning and dysfunctioning. We explore the continuum theory of emotional reactions, focus on ways in which emotional disorders are maintained, look at building a therapeutic relationship based on collaborative empiricism, promote guided discovery through Socratic questioning and help clients to become self-therapists.

Introduction

Cognitive behaviour therapy (CBT) is a generic term that refers to more than 20 approaches within this tradition (Mahoney and Lyddon, 1988). CT approaches focus on the way thoughts influence feelings and behaviour. The leading approach within this field is Beck's (1976) cognitive therapy (CT) which is the subject of this book.

CT was developed by Aaron T. Beck, an American psychiatrist, at the University of Pennsylvania in the early 1960s (Beck, 1995). CT examines the idiosyncratic meanings that individuals assign to events in order to understand their emotional and behavioural reactions to these events. For example, three people have to re-apply for their jobs within the same company: the first person is anxious because he believes the company is looking for a way to get rid of him; the second person is angry because she believes that one job interview should be sufficient; the third person feels hurt because he believes he is being treated unfairly after years of loyal service. The situation is the same for all three but each emotional reaction is largely determined by the individual's appraisal of the situation and not by the situation itself; if the situation determined our feelings then we should all feel anxious, for example, about public speaking because the situation would not allow us to feel in any other way. A concise way of understanding CT is: we feel the way we think (Burns, 1980).

CT developed at a time when the dominant approaches in therapy were psychoanalysis and behaviourism. Unlike psychoanalysis, CT does not interpret clients' unconscious processes (e.g. repression) but focuses on exploring their conscious and preconscious (currently unaware of but accessible with therapist prompting) patterns of thinking. Clients themselves provide the raw cognitive data that form the basis of the therapeutic exchange. Unlike behaviour therapy's emphasis on environmental determinism, CT stresses individual free will and the capacity to change through cognitive restructuring. Reality testing is directed at clients' thinking and not at their overt behaviours.

Beck's approach initially focused on research into, and clinical treatment of, depression but over the past 30 years CT has been applied to an ever-increasing number of clinical problems and populations. These include anxiety (Beck, Emery and Greenberg, 1985), substance abuse (Beck et al., 1993), eating disorders (Fairburn and Cooper, 1989), schizophrenia (Perris, 1989), obsessive–compulsive disorder (Salkovskis and Kirk, 1989), couples (Dattilio and Padesky, 1990), psychiatric inpatients (Wright et al., 1993), children and adolescents (Reinecke, Dattilio and Freeman, 1996) and personality disorders (Beck, Freeman and Associates, 1990).

Theory

Subjective construction of reality

This is seeing the world through the client's eyes. This subjective viewpoint or self-talk is usually revealed through therapist questioning (tapping the internal communications, as Beck (1976) calls it). Clients can often be puzzled as to why they respond in certain ways to specific situations. For example, a man who wanted a job promotion eventually got it but became so anxious he refused to go work. Why? As Beck (1976, p. 26) says: 'When a person is able to fill in the gap between an activating event and the emotional consequences, the puzzling reaction becomes understandable'. In this example, the man reveals that wanting a job promotion was only to prove to himself and his wife that he was still ambitious; when he actually got it he dreaded the pressure and new responsibilities that would be 'heaped on me'. Training clients to tap into their self-talk is a key task of CT therapists and the indispensable question that facilitates such training is: 'What was going through your mind at that moment to make you feel ... ?'

Information-processing model

Beck's approach is based on an information-processing model 'which posits that during psychological distress a person's thinking becomes more rigid and distorted, judgements become overgeneralized and absolute, and the person's basic beliefs about the self and the world become fixed' (Weishaar, 1996, p. 188). In other words, when we are experiencing emotional distress, our normal information-processing abilities tend to become faulty because we introduce a consistently negative bias into our thinking. For example, a depressed person perceives his wife's and friends' efforts to cheer him up as 'doomed to failure because I'm beyond all help. They know that but they won't admit it.'

Common information-processing errors or distortions in emotional disturbance include:

- All-or-nothing thinking: situations are viewed in 'either/or' terms rather than in a more balanced and realistic way (for example, a student thinks 'either I'm number one or I'm a flop' about his examination performance).
- Mindreading: thinking you can discern the thoughts of others without any accompanying evidence (for example, a lecturer who catches one of his students looking out of the window while he is leading a tutorial decides she must be thinking about him 'He's really boring').
- Labelling: instead of labelling the behaviour, you attach the label to yourself (for example, 'Because I failed my driving test for the second time, this means I'm a failure').
- 'Should' and 'must' statements: demands and commands made on ourselves, others and the world and the 'terrible' consequences when they are not met (for example, 'I must get this job because if I don't my life will be awful without it').
- Emotional reasoning: assuming that your disturbed or strong feelings are facts (for example, 'I feel that my friends are stabbing me in the back, so it must be true'). (The first part of the example is actually a thought, not a feeling. The differences between thoughts and feelings are explained in Chapter 3.)

Teaching clients how to identify and examine such distorted or erroneous thinking facilitates the return to information processing that is more accurate, flexible and relative (non-absolute) in its appraisals of events. Gilbert (1992) takes issue with the word 'error' as this implies there is a correct way of thinking; to sidestep this thorny issue, he suggests the use of non-contentious expressions such as 'anxious thoughts' or 'depressing thoughts' instead of 'cognitive errors'.

Structural organization of thinking

Three cognitive levels are examined in CT:

- Automatic thoughts.
- Underlying assumptions.
- Core beliefs (also known as 'schemas', a technical term).

Automatic thoughts

These are thoughts that appear to come rapidly, automatically and involuntarily when a person is in a negative frame of mind and are linked to specific emotional reactions (such as depression or anxiety). Automatic thoughts usually lie outside of immediate awareness though they can be quickly brought into consciousness. Gilbert (1992, p. 35) calls them 'pop-up thoughts ... [and] are not arrived at through reflective reasoning'. Automatic thoughts can be triggered by external events (for example, coming late to a meeting) or internal ones (a pounding heart). For example, a therapist whose client does not keep a second appointment might experience anxiety because he believes 'She doesn't think I'm any good and that's why she didn't come back. She's probably complaining to her GP that I can't help her. He might not send me any more referrals. I'll never make it as a therapist'. Automatic thoughts are situation-specific and are the easiest cognitions to access.

Negative appraisals of situations can also occur in the form of images (for example, a socially anxious person has images of making a fool of herself by stumbling over words when introduced to others and being laughed at because of it). If a client says 'I'm not thinking anything' in a particular situation, probe instead for the presence of images connected to the client's feelings about the situation. Probing for negative images about events should be a routine part of the assessment process, as this helps clients to become more aware that their negative automatic thoughts can occur in pictures as well as words (Beck, 1995). As part of a treatment programme, clients can learn to replace distressing imagery with coping imagery.

Underlying assumptions

These are the often unarticulated conditional assumptions which guide our behaviour, set the standards we must achieve or provide rules we must follow (for example, (positive assumption) 'If I please others, then they'll like me'; (negative assumption) 'If I don't please others, then they will reject me'). (As you can see from these two examples, underlying assumptions are usually identified by their 'if... then' construction.) Rules are expressed in 'should' statements: 'I should strive never to let anyone down'. As long as the terms of these rules, standards and positive assumptions are being met, individuals remain relatively stable and productive (Fennell, 1997).

These assumptions and rules are the means by which individuals hope to avoid coming 'face-to-face' with their core negative beliefs (such as 'I'm useless'); they are not formulated to help individuals examine and change these core beliefs. If these rules are not adhered to or assumptions are unmet, individuals are vulnerable to emotional distress when negative core beliefs are activated (for example, a man becomes increasingly distraught when he realizes that his girlfriend is going to leave him despite his attempts always to please her; her departure will prove his worthlessness). Underlying assumptions are cross-situational.

Core beliefs (schemas)

These are fundamental beliefs about ourselves, others and the world and make sense of our experience. We usually have both positive core beliefs (such as 'I'm successful') and negative core beliefs ('I'm a failure'). Core beliefs are usually formed through early learning experiences and become instrumental in shaping our outlook. In emotional disturbance, rigid, unconditional and overgeneralized negative core beliefs (such as 'I'm repulsive to everyone') are activated and then process information in a biased way that confirms the core belief and disconfirms any contradictory evidence. Once the disturbance has passed or ameliorated, negative core beliefs become deactivated or return to their latent state and a more positive outlook is re-established (clients with personality disorders may have their negative core beliefs activated most of the time). Beck (1995) suggests that negative core beliefs fall into two broad categories: helplessness (e.g. 'I'm weak') and unlovability (e.g. 'I'm unattractive'). If enduring constructive change is to occur in clients' lives then negative core beliefs need to be uncovered and modified.

The work of Jeffrey Young (1994; Young and Behary, 1998) has been influential in understanding the operation of core beliefs (schemas). According to Young (1994) core beliefs are perpetuated in three main ways:

- Schema maintenance – thinking and behaving in ways that reinforce core beliefs (for example, a woman who sees herself as worthless chooses partners who treat her badly, thereby confirming her view of her worthlessness).
- Schema avoidance – seeking ways to avoid activating core beliefs and the painful feelings associated with them (for example, a man who sees himself as unattractive does not ask women out because he fears rejection and the ensuing depression).

- Schema compensation – acting in ways that appear to contradict the core belief (for example, a woman who sees herself as a failure takes on many tasks to prove the opposite). Cognitive, behavioural and emotive techniques are employed to examine and modify dysfunctional schemas, thereby helping to halt this perpetuation process (for further discussion of core beliefs, see Chapter 5).

How are automatic thoughts, underlying assumptions or rules and core beliefs linked? Core beliefs form the templates for processing incoming information about self, others and the world; underlying assumptions, derived from core beliefs, provide the basis for our conduct in life; automatic thoughts occur in situations where the assumptions or rules are not achieved. (For example, an individual who sees himself as a failure does not live up his rule of working hard to stave off defeat and is flooded with negative automatic thoughts reflecting his failure schema when his first article is rejected for publication: 'The article was obviously rubbish. All that work for nothing. What's the point of trying hard?'). The usual treatment strategy in CT is early therapeutic intervention at the level of negative automatic thoughts (NATs) to produce symptom-relief and then moving on to underlying beliefs to effect longer-term change.

Reciprocal interaction of thoughts, feelings, behaviour, physiology and environment

CT is not a linear model of emotional functioning whereby a thought about a situation leads to a feeling/physiological response, which then leads to a behaviour. Each one of these elements or components is capable of influencing the others in an interactive cycle. Greenberger and Padesky (1995) suggest these are the five components found in any problem. For example, a woman who loses her job (environment) sees herself as a failure (thought), feels depressed (emotion), withdraws from social activities (behaviour) and complains of constant tiredness (physiology). Any change in one of these components (such as a gradual return to social functioning) can initiate changes in the other four components.

In CT, the usual 'way in' to start the change process is by examining clients' negative thoughts (for example, 'Are there other ways of viewing job loss apart from self-condemnation?') as these have a crucial impact on feelings, behaviour, physiology and how clients respond to environmental stressors. In the above example, when the client begins to view job loss as part of the employment cycle, her depressed mood lifts, energy levels increase and the client starts updating her CV in preparation for more job applications.

Content–specificity hypothesis (Beck, 1976)

This proposes that emotional disorders have a specific cognitive content or theme running through them. For example, devaluation or loss in depression, danger or threat in anxiety, situationally specific dangers in phobia, transgression in anger, unwarranted intrusion in paranoia. These themes are tied to Beck's (1976) concept of the 'personal domain', that is anything that individuals consider important in their lives. Some examples may help to explain this relationship:

- An individual who prides herself on being a successful businesswoman becomes depressed when her company goes into liquidation as she concludes 'My work is my life and without it, I'm nothing'.
- A man becomes anxious that his sexual prowess will be ridiculed if he is unable to satisfy a highly sexed woman.
- A woman who enjoys peace and quiet in her life becomes very angry when her next door neighbour plays his music very loudly.

How an individual responds emotionally to events 'depends on whether he perceives events as adding to, subtracting from, endangering, or impinging upon his domain' (Beck, 1976, p. 56). Weishaar (1996) states that the content-specificity hypothesis was validated empirically by a number of studies in the 1980s (e.g. Beck et al., 1987; Clark, Beck and Brown, 1989).

Cognitive vulnerability

This refers to 'idiosyncratic vulnerabilities' that predispose a person to psychological disturbance. What may precipitate disturbance in one individual (perhaps the loss of a job) proves non-disturbance-inducing in another. The interplay between various factors (such as childhood experiences or traumas, inadequate coping mechanisms, rigid attitudes, developmental history or personality differences) determines which life events will trigger maladaptive reactions. Beck (1987) hypothesized two broad personality types who would be prone to experience depression after a perceived loss: 'sociotropy' and 'autonomy'.

> The autonomous individual gets his satisfaction from independence, freedom and personal achievement, while the sociotropic individual is dependent on social gratifications, such as affection, company and approval. (Blackburn and Davidson, 1995, p. 29)

Depression may be triggered in autonomous individuals if they are blocked from attaining important goals, whereas depression may occur in sociotropic individuals if they become socially isolated.

Maladaptive beliefs and assumptions relating to themes of personal danger or threat may present a vulnerability to anxiety (Beck, Emery and Greenberg, 1985). Danger or threat beliefs form a bias in how individuals process incoming information. This bias predisposes individuals to systematically overestimate the danger inherent in particular situation(s) and underestimate their ability to cope with these situation(s). (For example, a man who believes he cannot be happy without a relationship views every unexplained action on his wife's part as evidence she is going to leave him and he will 'fall apart' if she does.)

Continuum of emotional reactions

CT suggests continuity between 'normal' emotional and behavioural reactions to life events and exaggerated emotional and behavioural reactions found in psychopathology (disturbances in thoughts, feelings and behaviours). As Weishaar and Beck (1986, p. 65) explain:

> The cognitive content of syndromes (e.g. anxiety disorders, depression) have the same theme (danger or loss, respectively) as found in 'normal' experience, but cognitive distortions are more extreme and, consequently, so are affect and behaviour.

Also, physiological reactions would be similar if the perceived threat was psychosocial (such as fear of making mistakes in front of others) or physical (being threatened in the street).

Normal and exaggerated emotional reactions to events are characterized by what Beck et al. (1979) call 'mature' (flexible) and 'primitive' (absolute) thinking, respectively. (For example, a mature response to the loss of a relationship might be 'time heals', whereas a primitive response might conclude 'I'll never get over it'). Explaining to clients this continuum of cognitive–emotive–behavioural reactions to life events can help to remove some of the stigma from the experience of emotional disturbance and thereby normalize it (Weishaar, 1993).

Acquisition of emotional disturbance

CT does not claim that dysfunctional thinking causes emotional distress; rather that it forms an integral part of this distress. There are a number of factors which predispose individuals to psychological distress including genetic, developmental, environmental, cultural, physical, familial and personality. The interactions of these factors help form idiosyncratic assumptions and beliefs about oneself, others and the world. (For example, a child who was smacked and criticized every time he cried developed the rigid belief 'I must not show any weaknesses to any one because if I do, this will prove I'm inadequate' which then helped to shape his relationships with others.) Such a dysfunctional belief leaves individuals vulnerable to, for example, anxiety if they fear they might reveal a weakness, and depression and shame if they do.

Maintenance of emotional disturbance

Although dysfunctional thinking does not cause emotional problems, it does play a central role in maintaining them (Beck, Emery and Greenberg, 1985). Once the dysfunctional core belief (schema) has been activated, it produces the cognitive shift away from more positive or adaptive beliefs and begins systematically to distort incoming information about the situation in order to fit and thereby maintain the activated core belief. Following on from the above example, the individual was unable to meet a tight deadline at work and thereby revealed a 'weakness' to his colleagues. All further tasks undertaken were viewed through the distorting lens of his personal inadequacy. Even if a client's emotional distress 'is conceptualized as resulting from environmental and biological stressors, a cognitive focus would be an important part of the treatment' (Padesky and Greenberger, 1995, p. 4).

Behaviour plays an important role in maintaining emotional distress as individuals act in ways that support their dysfunctional beliefs. For example, a person who sees herself as weak and unable to cope on her own acts in a 'helpless' way by expecting her partner to tell her what to do and make decisions for her. Behavioural change would involve acting against her dysfunctional beliefs by making her own decisions and thereby beginning 'to stand on my own feet'.

Practice

The role of emotion in CT

The word 'cognitive' may give the impression that therapists focus on thoughts to the exclusion of feelings. This is untrue as emotions are the starting point for therapeutic intervention – after all, clients usually come to therapy complaining of how they feel, not about what they think. Beck et al. (1979, p. 35) stress the importance of being empathic with clients' painful feelings 'as well as to be able to identify his faulty cognitions and the linkage between his negative thoughts and negative feelings'. The conduct of CT is pointless if emotions are not activated as it will become a purely cerebral exchange and key 'hot' (emotionally charged) cognitions will not be revealed.

The presence of affect in therapy is required to undertake cognitive restructuring (for example, an individual who procrastinates over starting a college essay is asked to imagine putting pen to paper in order to release (in this case) his anxiogenic thoughts of failure and disgrace when his essay receives only a mediocre grade); once these thoughts have been exposed, modification of them can begin. Dattilio and Padesky (1990, p. 2) state that 'the therapist should be skilled at eliciting affect if the client does not express it spontaneously'.

The role of behaviour

Behavioural patterns help to maintain emotional distress and dysfunctional thinking. For example, Clark (1986) suggests that people who experience recurring panic attacks have an enduring tendency to interpret catastrophically their bodily sensations such as dizziness and unsteadiness – 'I'm going to faint!' What prevents clients from re-evaluating their catastrophic thinking in a more realistic way is the operation of safety behaviours (Salkovskis, 1991). These behaviours avert the perceived imminent catastrophe through avoidance action: so in the above example, the person who is afraid of fainting sits down or holds on to something. As Wells (1997, p. 6) remarks:

> Whilst the behaviour may relieve anxiety it unintentionally preserves the belief in the catastrophe. Under these conditions each panic becomes an example of a 'near miss' rather than a disconfirmation of belief, and danger may seem subsequently more evident.

Dropping safety behaviours, whether overt or covert, is a key behavioural strategy in treating anxiety disorders in order to effect cognitive change. Behavioural methods of change have always been central to the practice of CT (Dattilio and Padesky, 1990).

Developing a therapeutic relationship

In CT, a therapeutic relationship is constructed, in part, on the basis of Rogers' (1957) core conditions of counselling: empathy, genuineness, respect, warmth and unconditional positive regard. Beck et al. (1979, p. 45) state 'that these characteristics in themselves are necessary but not sufficient to produce an optimum therapeutic effect'. By demonstrating these and other therapeutic qualities, the therapist 'is helping to develop a milieu in which the specific cognitive change techniques can be applied most efficiently' (Beck et al., 1979, p. 46). These change techniques are 'applied most efficiently' by therapists and clients working as a team or co-collaborators in the problem-solving process (see below for a discussion of collaborative empiricism).

The focus in the early development of CT was on the therapeutic relationship as a vehicle 'for the execution of techniques. Only later was the relationship to be viewed as an intervention tool in itself' (Blackburn and Twaddle, 1996, p. 7). One example of the relationship as an intervention tool is its use with clients who have personality disorders where the relationship becomes 'a schema laboratory in which the client can safely evaluate maladaptive core beliefs [e.g. "Nobody can be trusted"]' (Padesky and Greenberger, 1995, p. 123). This 'relationship as laboratory' metaphor also encourages the testing and development of alternative and adaptive schemas (such as 'Some people can be trusted sometimes').

Collaborative empiricism (Beck et al., 1979)

This term refers to clients and therapists working together as a team to understand and tackle clients' emotional and behavioural problems; clients are actively engaged in the problem-solving process. 'Empiricism' means the process of reality-testing clients' thoughts, assumptions and beliefs. These cognitions are viewed as hypotheses about reality rather than as facts (clients, of course, can and do cling on to their beliefs as indisputable facts). Evidence collected from such reality testing (for example, behavioural experiments conducted to test a client's assumption, 'If I ask my friend for a favour, he will reject me') is evaluated to determine if it confirms or contradicts clients' hypotheses and 'by this means, clients are encouraged both to view their thoughts as personal constructs of reality and to build their skills in evaluating their validity' (Nelson-Jones, 1995, p. 312). Through this process of collaborative empiricism, clients can learn to become 'personal scientists'.

Guided discovery and Socratic questioning

Guided discovery is the process whereby therapists act as a guide to help clients elicit, examine and reality-test their dysfunctional thoughts and beliefs, aid the development of more adaptive and balanced responses to their problems and discern themes in their thinking (such as the need for approval). This process is facilitated by Socratic or open-ended questioning which 'opens up' clients' closed patterns of thinking associated with their problems and encourages the development of new perspectives from which to address these problems. For example, Socratic questioning of an anxious client might include:

'What was going through your mind at that moment to make you feel anxious when your boyfriend turned up late?'

'What did you do?'

'Are there any other explanations apart from he is seeing someone else?'

'Let's assume the worst, what if he is seeing someone else?'

'What does that mean about you?'

'How would you like to see yourself instead of your present self-image of worth-lessness?'

Guided discovery through Socratic questioning is not about arguing, disputing, tripping clients up or telling them what to think – they are unlikely to be convinced if you just 'hand them' an explanation for their worries ('I'm sure you're not a bad mother: if you were, would your children seem so happy and content? Of course not'). As Beck et al. (1979, p. 300) state 'The major premise in cognitive therapy is to speak from the data – not attempt to convince the patient through force of argument'.

Socratic questioning can give the impression that the therapist has an end-point in mind (such as to prove to the client that panic attacks will not lead to insanity), but Padesky (1993a) argues that the best form of guided discovery assumes there are no preconceived answers or known end-points. On the other hand, Wells (1997, p. 56) suggests that:

My own view on guided discovery and the Socratic dialogue ... is that a combin-ation of both knowing where to go, but allowing time to explore the patient's evidence for thoughts and for the patient to generate solutions is desirable.

Clients learn the techniques of guided discovery as part of their developing roles as self-therapists.

Generalization of in-session therapeutic change (Vallis, Howes and Miller, 1991)

This refers to the homework tasks that clients are encouraged to carry out between sessions based on what has been discussed in the session. With CT's emphasis on reality-testing, homework is the logical way of carrying out this function. Homework provides opportunities for not only testing maladaptive beliefs but also for thinking and behaving differently in problematic contexts. Much of clients' confidence in becoming self-therapists is gained through homework. Burns (1989, p. 545) suggests 'that compliance with self-help assignments may be the most important predictor of therapeutic success'. Homework tasks are reviewed at the beginning of the next session as part of agenda-setting. If you or your clients do not like the word 'homework' then choose whatever term is more appealing (for example, 'real-life activities', 'outside session tasks').

Openness

As CT practice is based on collaboration, therapy is open and explicit about 'what is going on'. For example conceptualizations of clients' presenting problems are discussed with them, therapists' hypotheses are open to confirmation, modification or rejection, based on incoming information (do not seek information that only confirms your hypotheses). Therapists' mistakes are admitted and clients can and do suggest solutions when therapy gets stalled. CT rejects any hidden agendas on the part of therapists as this would undermine the spirit and practice of collaboration (Blackburn and Twaddle, 1996).

Case conceptualization

This refers to understanding clients' problems within the cognitive model of emotional disorders. The primary focus is on the cognitive–behavioural factors that maintain clients' emotional difficulties and the underlying beliefs and assumptions, personality vulnerabilities, past traumas and life experiences that predispose individuals to experience their particular problems. Past and present interact to produce an idiosyncratic clinical picture of clients' presenting problems. From this conceptualization, a treatment plan is derived to guide therapy. A case conceptualization is viewed as tentative as it is subject to revision and refinement as further information about clients' problems is revealed. Case conceptualization is also known as 'case formulation' (see Chapter 2).

Focus on the here and now

The primary therapeutic focus of CT is on the factors maintaining clients' problems:

> ... little attention is paid to childhood recollections except to clarify present observations. (Beck et al., 1979, p. 7)

For example, if a client says 'My parents made me feel like a failure as a child', the therapist can ask 'Do you still see yourself as a failure today?' Historical factors that contributed to or are 'seen' to be the cause of current problems (such as lack of parental love) occurred in an irrevocable past and therefore cannot be changed or modified. In addition, 'knowledge about problem acquisition is unlikely even to improve the treatment of a disorder' (Bond, 1998, p. 84).

Having said all that, Beck (1995, p. 7) suggests that:

> attention shifts to the past in three circumstances: when the patient expresses a strong predilection to do so; when work directed towards current problems

produces little or no cognitive, behavioral, and emotional change; or when the therapist judges that it is important to understand how and when important dysfunctional ideas originated and how these ideas affect the patient today.

Obviously, you will need to present to your clients a clinical rationale for the mainly ahistorical (here and now) stance of CT.

Becoming a self-therapist

This means that as clients' problem-solving abilities increase, you can become less active in guiding therapy. The transition from client to self-therapist is greatly facilitated by homework or between-session assignments as clients gain competence and confidence in tackling their problems. The CT model of emotional disorders is a psycho-educational one, so clients can learn the model for both present and future problem-solving.

Additional features of CT practice

CT employs a highly structured approach in order to make the most efficient use of the time clients spend in therapy. Other features of this structured approach include:

Active-directive

This is a focused approach that actively guides clients to the salient aspects of their presenting problems and is deemed to be more effective in helping clients change than a passive or non-directive style of intervention. Therapists are active in, among other activities, collecting assessment data in order to arrive at a cognitive conceptualization of clients' problems and directing them towards the connections between their thoughts, feelings and behaviours.

Socialization into CT

Wells (1997) describes this process as 'selling' the cognitive model to clients as an effective means of tackling their problems. Socialization includes presenting the cognitive model, encouraging clients to assume the role of co-collaborator in their treatment, developing a conceptualization of their problems and a treatment plan based on it, and outlining the expected course of therapy.

Agenda setting

This is a business-like approach to therapy but is not carried out in an impersonal way. Clients and therapists agree which topics are to be put on the agenda for discussion in each session; this encourages each participant in the therapeutic exchange to be problem-focused rather than letting therapy meander. The usual items placed on the agenda are reviewing homework, topics to be discussed in the present session, negotatiating new homework and obtaining feedback at the end of the session.

Feedback

This is not only obtained at the end of a session but also during it. Feedback is two way: clients are invited to comment on therapy and therapists (for example, 'Why do we need an agenda?', 'Why can't I just talk about whatever I want?', 'You're not giving me enough time to respond to your questions.'). Therapists seek to correct any misunderstandings clients may have about therapy and check their clients' understanding of points that have been made (for example, 'Could you put in your own words how panic attacks are made worse by the way you think about them?'). It is important that you react non-defensively or without irritation to clients' feedback that is critical of you as this might indicate to clients that only positive feedback is acceptable or solicted. Feedback is an important part of the openness and collaboration of CT.

Use of a problem list

Clients do not usually present in therapy with a single, self-contained problem; more likely they will have several problems which are itemized in order of priority (this does not automatically mean that the most troubling will be tackled first). A problem list reassures clients that each problem will be dealt with or 'ticked off' but obviously not all at the same time.

Goals for change

For each problem identified, a specific and concrete goal needs to be agreed (for example, a client who says he is housebound due to panic attacks states his goal as the 'ability to get to the local shops on my own'). Accepting vague goals is discouraged as they will prove difficult to measure (for example, 'I want to be more in control of my life.'). What prevents clients from being more in control of their lives? Each factor that prevents or hinders increased control may be translated into a goal, such as 'I put off making important decisions in case they turn out badly' can become a timescale for making a decision and developing a coping strategy if the consequences of the decision turn out to be disadvantageous.

Relapse prevention

Perhaps more accurately described as 'relapse reduction'. Further episodes of emotional distress can and do occur once therapy has finished. These episodes are often triggered by the reactivation of core dysfunctional beliefs which may have been modified to some extent but still pose a threat in particular situations. During the latter stages of CT, attention is turned to relapse prevention strategies to deal with setbacks after formal therapy has ended. Follow-up appointments may be arranged to check on progress and are a further 'boost' to the maintenance of treatment gains.

Time-limited approach

This means that an approximate, not specific, timescale can be advanced for the length of therapy, rather than being open-ended (clients frequently ask 'How long will I have to be in therapy?'). Beck (1995) suggests that uncomplicated anxiety and depression disorders usually require between four and fourteen treatment sessions. The actual time spent in therapy could be between one and four months. For chronic cases, such as personality disorders, 'the consensus seems to be that effective treatment... takes one and a half to four years' (Scott, Stradling and Dryden, 1995, p. 9).

Misconceptions about CT

The following are some of the common misconceptions held about the theory and practice of CT.

CT is just common sense

This usually means that CT appears straightforward to apply because it simply encourages clients to think realistically about their problems and thereby stop blowing things out of proportion. Beck's (1976) book, *Cognitive Therapy and the Emotional Disorders*, contains a chapter called 'Common sense and beyond' in which he acknowledges that common sense may be used 'as a framework for understanding and changing attitudes and behavior' (Beck, 1976, p. 14), but it fails to understand or solve the 'puzzling' emotional disorders. Common sense is not idiosyncratically based (i.e. seen through the eyes of clients) and therefore cannot be used either as a blueprint for understanding their problems or as a treatment plan derived from them. Often, uncommon sense or detective work is required to unravel the mysteries of clients' presenting problems and to devise ways of tackling them.

CT is superficial or only applies a sticking plaster to clients' problems

This assumes that CT investigates only surface cognitions (i.e. automatic thoughts) and neglects deeper problems or core concerns. Although automatic thoughts are the initial targets of change in order to effect symptom relief, a clinical rationale would be presented to clients to work on underlying beliefs if longer-term and enduring change is to be achieved and relapses are to be avoided or minimized. Obviously, clients make the final decision about the issues they want to work on or the depth of change they wish to achieve; however, it is important to remember that what might be considered 'superficial change' to the therapist may be seen as very significant by the client.

CT is about positive thinking

A student recently said (to the author, MN) that CT cannot help clients when things go wrong in their lives 'because you lot (CTers) only teach clients to think positively about everything'. CT is not a therapy based on 'the power of positive thinking', but is based on 'the power of realistic thinking' (Beck et al., 1979). Therapists do not try to persuade clients that painful events are actually 'blessings in disguise' but help them to identify and correct any inaccurate inferences they are making about these events. In this way, clients may learn to adapt constructively to these events without having to 'feel good' about them.

CT can be used only with clients who are articulate and intelligent

This might seem to be the case with the emphasis of CT on introspection and reality testing, but Beck (1995, p. 2) reports on research which 'found that cognitive therapy is effective for patients with different levels of education, income, and background'. For this to occur, ensure that CT is tailored to clients' requirements rather than clients being 'fitted into' the model. CT is used with supposedly 'unsuitable' populations, such as those with learning disabilities (Kroese, Dagnan and Loumidis, 1997).

CT is not interested in the past, only the present

As stated earlier in this chapter, the past is not neglected if deemed to be clinically relevant in understanding and/or tackling clients' problems, but the 'focus is not so much on what was but rather on what is and what maintains or reinforces dysfunctional behaviour' (Dattilio and Freeman, 1992, p. 9).

Note on terminology

The terms 'maladaptive' and 'dysfunctional' are found everywhere in CT literature, including this book, and the use of 'irrational' is avoided. As Weishaar (1993, p. 119) explains:

> Beck eschews the word 'irrational' in reference to maladaptive thoughts, for at one time in the person's life these beliefs made sense. Dysfunctional beliefs contribute to psychological disorders because they interfere with normal cognitive processing, not because they are irrational.

It might be better in some cases to ditch CT jargon and use more client-friendly terms, such as 'self-defeating' or 'unhelpful' when referring to distorted thinking.

In this chapter we have discussed key aspects of CT theory and practice, and equipped with this overview, we now turn our attention to the assessment of clients' presenting problems.

Chapter Two
Assessment and
Socialization into CT

In this chapter, we look at the assessment process based upon a case conceptualization approach. Three key areas that inform the conceptualization are:

- A detailed description of the presenting problem.
- An ABC cross-sectional analysis of the problem.
- The historical context of the problem, including underlying assumptions and core beliefs associated with it.

Alongside the assessment we describe socializing clients into therapy in order for them to understand the cognitive model, as well as their own expected role in CT.

Introducing clients to CT

During the first session of CT it is important to teach your clients the relationship between thoughts and feelings; in other words, to teach the 'cognitive model'. Your clinical judgement can determine when to introduce the model in the session. For example, if your client attends the appointment in an anxious state it might be profitable to tease out then and there her anxiogenic thinking and how it can be restructured to reduce her anxiety:

Therapist: What thoughts are going through your mind at the moment to make you feel anxious about coming here?

Client: Maybe you'll think I'm a hopeless case.

Therapist: So you think that I might think you are a hopeless case (client nods). And if I do think that . . .?

Client: Then I'll never get any better and my life won't be much fun.

Therapist: Now let's say that I can definitely help you, you will get better because I'm very good at my job. Would that have any impact on how you feel?

Client: It would do if I believed it.

Therapist: And do you believe it?

Client: I'm certainly prepared to give you the benefit of the doubt.

Therapist: Does that change in any way how you feel at the moment?

Client: I'm feeling a little less anxious now because maybe there is a way forward with my problems after all. You've given me some confidence.

Therapist: Good. The point of this dialogue is to show you how our thoughts (tapping head) influence our feelings. This is the essence of the cognitive model that I want to apply to your problems.

Another method of teaching the model is suggested by Blackburn and Davidson (1995, p. 55) who advise that, after you have gained some understanding of your client's problems, you use 'a didactic approach to explain the *cognitive therapy model* to ensure a basic *understanding* and future *collaboration* from the patient' (italics in original). Make your illustration of the model as concrete as possible. For example:

Therapist: How someone thinks about events determines how they feel about them. For example, a person is waiting for a telephone call regarding the outcome of a job interview. He is thinking 'I won't get it because they thought I was a poor candidate, the worst of the lot'. He feels anxious and decides to go out to avoid hearing the 'bad news'. While out walking he says to himself 'You stupid fool running away like this. Get back to the house at once'. He feels angry and embarrassed and hurries homewards. Putting the key in the door, he thinks he hears the phone ringing and rushes inside declaring 'I bet I've got the job after all!' He is momentarily elated. The phone is not ringing and he reflects 'that no news is good news'. He is now emotionally calmer and busies himself with other tasks rather than focusing on the impending phone call.

You can then relate this illustration to clients' presenting problems and ask them if they can make any connections between their thoughts and feelings. Also, does the cognitive model make sense to clients and can they see its usefulness in helping them to tackle their problems? Teaching the cognitive model is not a 'one off' but occurs repeatedly throughout the course of therapy. The best way to teach the model is probably through examples derived from clients' personal experiences.

Case conceptualization

Case conceptualization is based on a highly individualized under-standing of clients' problems within a cognitive framework: it hypothe-sizes how clients' problems are being maintained and the underlying factors that predispose them to experience these problems. Persons (1989) describes this process in terms of 'overt difficulties' (such as depression, panic attacks, procrastination) and 'underlying psycholog-ical mechanisms' (for example, dysfunctional beliefs and assumptions). An underlying belief such as 'Nothing I achieve is ever good enough', would be largely responsible for a client's overt problems of general dissatisfaction with his life and depressed mood. Freeman (1992, p. 14) states that 'the highest-order clinical skill is the ability to develop treat-ment conceptualizations'.

A case conceptualization approach differs from a psychiatric diagnosis by trying to understand clients' internal reality rather than attaching labels to them (for example, social phobia); describing the clinical features of a psychiatric disorder does not tell you much about the person. For example, two clients may be labelled as having social phobia and therefore appear to have identical problems, but a case conceptualization might reveal different reasons for the development and maintenance of the problem and thereby the need for different treatment plans (Bruch, 1998).

The use of measures

Measures are used to assess the severity of clients' presenting problems and act as a baseline for determining, among other factors, clients' progress during the course of therapy. Two of the most commonly used measures in CT are the *Beck Depression Inventory* (BDI) (Beck et al., 1961) and the *Beck Anxiety Inventory* (BAI) (Beck et al., 1988). The BDI is a 21-item self-report inventory which provides a rapid assessment of the severity of clients' depression, including the degree of hopelessness experienced and the presence of suicidal ideas. Clients are asked to describe how they have been feeling over the past week, including the day of administration of the BDI.

The BAI is a 21-item self-report scale measuring the severity of individ-uals' cognitive and physiological responses to anxiety. Clients are asked to report their symptoms over the last week, including the day of administra-tion of the BAI. Inventories such as these are given to clients before the start of a session and can usually provide a guide, through the scoring, to how clients are responding to treatment (for example, a return to high scores usually indicates a setback or relapse). If progress is being made, the score should be coming down during the course of therapy.

Inventories are not used instead of clients' reports of their symptoms and progress, but are intended to be seen as one important indicator of therapeutic change.

Main features of assessment

Wells (1997) suggests three main areas to cover in the assessment interview:

- A detailed description of the presenting problem.
- An ABC cross-sectional analysis of the problem.
- An historical or longitudinal understanding of the problem.

These areas will be discussed in detail during the assessment phase, which can take one or more sessions to complete. Assessment never actually stops in CT as incoming information provides opportunities to refine data about clients' problems and allows repeated fine-tuning of the strategies and techniques for change. Assessment also includes drawing up a problem list, establishing goals for change, agreeing the first homework task (which might include collecting more assessment data) and gaining session feedback.

The client

Paul was a 34-year-old married man with two daughters, 9 and 7 years old. He had been referred by his GP for depression related to a recent business failure. He was currently taking anti-depressants. The referral letter said that Paul had gone to the GP only at his wife's insistence because he was very reluctant 'to let the world know about my failure'. When the therapist (MN) invited him into the office and motioned to him to sit in a chair, Paul moved to a chair furthest away and stared at the floor. His behaviour appeared to function as 'an interpersonal distance regulator' which Gilbert (1998) describes in his work on shame as a means of not letting others get too close and thereby becoming an object of scrutiny. MN sought evidence for his hypothesis that Paul was experiencing shame:

Therapist: Do you want to be here?

Paul: No.

Therapist: Where would you like to be?

Paul: I don't know, but not here with you staring at me.

Therapist: What does it mean to you to be here with me 'staring' at you?

[MN is attempting to understand the client's idiosyncratic view of the situation.]

Paul: (getting angry) That I can't cope. I'm weak and pathetic. No doubt, you see me like that too. What the hell do you know about me anyway?

Therapist: (quietly) Not much at the moment but I'd like to know more if you will let me. How do you feel at the moment?

Paul: (tears welling in his eyes) Very ashamed that I'm depressed. I should be able to cope with things in my life. Depression is for weaklings. I feel like leaving right now.

Therapist: How would that help you if you left now?

Paul: I'd feel better because I wouldn't be here being judged by you.

Therapist: If you left now would the judging stop?

Paul: What do you mean?

Therapist: Is it me judging you harshly or are you doing it to yourself? You said a moment ago you were 'weak and pathetic'.

Paul: Well I am.

Therapist: So if you walked out of here now, would you really feel any better?

Paul: No. I'd feel worse for running away and condemn myself even more.

Therapist: Do you think it might be better to stay and talk about your problems – bring them out into the open in other words – and see if you can trust me with them?

Paul: (warily) Maybe. Are you judging me?

Therapist: Only in the sense that I see a person in great distress whom I would like to help if given the chance.

Paul: Well, that sounds honest.

Therapist: Would you like to sit a bit closer now?

Paul: Okay.

A detailed description of the presenting problem

Paul described himself 'as a person who is always driven to succeed' and the failure of his recent business had 'wrecked everything'. He said he had been depressed for the last two months following his business failure. He found it an effort to do anything but he did help with chores around the house and continued to play with his children but not as much as before. His sleep pattern was fitful and he described lying awake at night worrying about his future. Normally fond of his food, his appetite was poor and he had lost weight. He spent a lot of time in the armchair brooding or, sometimes, pacing up and down 'wearing out the carpet'. He had lost interest in social activities because 'I don't want people to see me like this and I wouldn't enjoy it anyway'.

He had 'tinkered' with the idea of suicide 'as my family would be better off without me' but said it was never a serious possibility. He said he felt guilty for neglecting his wife and daughters, not being the main bread-winner and 'being a misery around the house'. When his parents and brothers phoned he put on a 'brave face as I haven't told them about the company going bust or my depression'. He said he made excuses why he could not visit them and feared their disapproval or even rejection if he revealed his problems to them. He also wondered if his wife secretly held him in contempt for 'being useless'.

Paul's problem list

- Lack of motivation.
- Lack of interest.
- 'I can't sleep properly.'
- 'I can't see a way forward.'
- Social avoidance.
- 'I'm afraid of telling my parents and brothers that I am depressed.'
- 'Seeing myself as weak and a failure.'
- 'I'm afraid that I will never get any job because of my business failure' ('Who will want me now?').

Paul's problem list was more extensive than this – it actually ran to over 20 items and initially seemed overwhelming – but it quickly became obvious that the problems identified were nearly all related to his depression. As Fennell (1989, p. 179) observes:

> The problem-list... imposes order on chaos. A mass of distressing experiences is reduced to a number of relatively specific difficulties. This process of 'problem-reduction' is crucial to the encouragement of hope, since it implies the possibility of control.

Goals

Once a problem list has been obtained (more problems may be added to the list later in therapy), individual problems need to be translated into measurable and observable goals for change. Paul said his goal for change was 'to get over this depression as quickly as possible'. Obviously, this goal was stated in general terms and therefore needed to be operationalized in clear and concrete ways. What would need to be happening in Paul's life to indicate that he was coming out of the depression? Paul suggested the following goals to tackle each problem on his list:

- 'I want to start being more active every day like helping more around the house and going out for walks.' As Burns (1989, p. 170) points out, action comes before motivation: 'You have to prime the pump by getting started whether you feel like it or not. Once you begin to accomplish something, it will often spur you on to do even more.'
- 'Take an interest in things like being able to read a newspaper every day, watching the television, talking to my wife more about her day.'
- 'To improve my sleeping pattern', e.g. avoid daytime naps, get up if he cannot sleep and engage in constructive activities until tiredness returns rather than tossing and turning and thereby increasing his nocturnal agitation.
- 'The way forward is to keep busy every day and not slouch about the house. Being busy means I'm achieving things and restoring a sense of purpose to my life.'
- 'To stop hiding away from the world and start participating in life again' (for example, accepting an invitation to a small dinner party).
- 'To tell my parents about my current problems when I'm feeling better and stronger.' (We agreed to return to a discussion of this goal after six sessions of therapy to determine 'if the time is right yet'.)
- 'I want to become more self-accepting, particularly when things go wrong or I don't measure up in some way. I want to stop calling myself weak or a failure and, instead, try and put things right in my life.' As Burns (1989, p. 109) states: 'Labels like "fool", "loser", "winner", "jerk", or "inferior person" are useless abstractions. It is far more productive to focus on what you *do* – and what you can do to learn and grow – than on what you *are*' (italics in original).
- 'Get myself back into the job market'. This seemed too ambitious as an initial goal given his current depressed state. Paul agreed. We decided to return to a discussion of this goal when Paul had shown some improvement.

Teaching the cognitive model

Therapist: Can I suggest that we spend the rest of this session looking at your current depression through the cognitive model and see if this makes any sense to you.

Paul: That's fine with me. I want things to start making sense.

Therapist: Is there anything else you would like to focus on in this session?

Paul: No. I think that's enough for the moment. I can't cope with too much at the present time.

Therapist: That's understandable, but please feel free to bring up other issues for discussion if anything comes to mind (client nods). We can start planning ways of working together to tackle your problems. At the end of the session we can discuss the first homework task and I would like to hear your initial impressions of therapy. Okay?

[The agenda is agreed jointly, MN invokes the collaborative 'we' and introduces Paul to the ideas of homework and session feedback.]

Paul: Okay. Can't hurt. (pause) Why do you say 'we can start planning. . .?' Aren't I the patient and you're supposed to get me better or something like that?

Therapist: Well, some forms of therapy might work like that, but in cognitive therapy we emphasize collaboration or working together as a team because I can't get you better on my own.

[MN deals with Paul's expectations of therapy and his role within it.]

Paul: I'm not sure I'm up to much collaboration at the moment.

Therapist: Well, we'll take it gently. You are already collaborating by providing information about your problems.

Paul: Hmm. I suppose that's true (smiles slightly).

Therapist: What was going through your mind just then when you smiled?

Paul: Maybe there is some light at the end of the tunnel after all.

Therapist: How do you feel at this precise moment?

Paul: A little better. Something similar happened this morning with one of my daughters. She said 'Please daddy get better quickly because I love you so much'. My spirits began to rise.

Therapist: These two examples show how our thoughts, no matter how fleeting, (tapping head) have a powerful impact on the way we feel.

Paul: Are you sure? As soon as she went upstairs my mood started to go down again. Why wasn't I still happy then? I wanted to be happy.

Therapist: Okay, let's write this example up on the whiteboard to make the cognitive model clearer.

An ABC analysis of Paul's depression

Paul provides the information for an ABC analysis: A = antecedents or situation; B = beliefs or thoughts; C = emotional and behavioural consequences. His thoughts (B) about the situation (A), not the situation itself, leads to the emotional and behavioural consequences experienced at C. The ABC model provides a simple but powerful demonstration of the effect of thought on feeling.

Table 2.1: An ABC analysis of Paul's depression

(A) Situation	(B) Beliefs/thoughts	(C) Consequences
Reflecting on daughter's comments and his inability to act on them	I've got such a wonderful daughter and I'm such a lousy father. Why can't I pull myself together? I'm pathetic for being like this.	*Emotion* Depression *Behaviour* Crying

Therapist: Does that example explain why you couldn't stay happy at that moment?

Paul: Yes it does.

Therapist: Could you explain it to me in your own words?

[MN elicits feedback from Paul to determine if he has understood the whiteboard example.]

Paul: Okay. Well, instead of using my daughter's comments as a starting point to help me get better, I immediately sank back into being very self-critical again.

Therapist: And what's the connection between what you think and how you feel?

Paul: (pointing at the whiteboard) Thinking those thoughts made me feel depressed again. It does make sense but are you saying my depression is totally caused by my thinking? It sounds so simple. Can it be that simple?

Therapist: I agree it sounds simple but identifying and changing those thoughts that are keeping you depressed isn't usually simple. Your depression is caused by many factors but thinking takes centre stage, so to speak, in maintaining your depression, keeping it going.

Paul: (nodding) Hmm. Most of the time I am thinking negatively.

Therapist: How does the world look through your eyes at the present time?

Paul: Bleak. I'm a failure, I can't find much enjoyment in my family life, nothing seems to interest me, everything is against me.

Therapist: And your future?

Paul: I can't see one.

Therapist: That's depression in a nutshell: everything, including yourself, is viewed in a highly negative way. That's the nature of the illness.

Paul: I can't seem to break out of it: the more I think about my failures, the worse I feel and the less I want to do, which then convinces me I am a failure . . . and so on. It just goes around in my head all day long.

Paul's comments in the last few exchanges reflect Beck's (1972; Beck et al., 1979) concept of the cognitive triad of depression: a negative view of oneself ('I'm a failure'); a negative view of the world ('Everything is against me'), and a negative view of the future ('I can't see one'). As the cognitive triad is one of the key features of the cognitive model of depression, therapists should 'look for evidence [of the triad] in the content of the patient's communications' (Blackburn and Davidson, 1995, p. 59).

Paul's last comments also demonstrate the vicious cycle in which clients can become trapped when thoughts, feelings and behaviour interact to maintain a depressed mood. Wills and Sanders (1997, p. 16) suggest that drawing:

> the 'vicious cycle' onto a piece of paper [or a whiteboard] can make the whole cycle seem more concrete and understandable – and *ipso facto* more likely to be open to change.

Use of a whiteboard enhances clients' understanding of the points being made or, alternatively, they grasp what the counsellor is explaining only when it is written down. As Nelson-Jones (1998, p. 78) observes:

> Many clients are more comfortable working in a visual modality rather than just a verbal modality.

Homework setting and session feedback

As the first session draws to a close, client and therapist discuss the first homework task to be undertaken:

Therapist: I mentioned the idea of homework earlier. This means you carrying on the work outside of therapy that we started within it.

Paul: I don't think I can do too much at the moment. What do you expect me to do?

Therapist: First, homework is about negotiation, not me imposing it on you. Second, the tasks will reflect what you feel you can carry out at any given time. I might suggest some reading to begin with about depression and how it can be tackled by using cognitive therapy.

[MN shows Paul *Feeling Good* by David Burns (1980), a self-help book.]

Or we can devise some daily tasks that you could carry out that might benefit you and help to lift your mood.

Paul: I could start with the book. You don't expect me to read all of it straightaway, do you?

Therapist: Just a few chapters will be fine. If anything strikes you as of particular interest, please note it down and we can discuss it at the next session. I'm writing down the homework task and will give you a copy of it in a moment.

Paul: Why do I need that?

Therapist: So there is no confusion at the next session over what was agreed when we discuss the task.

Paul: Okay.

Therapist: One last but important thing: it would be valuable for me to have your comments on this session.

[End of session feedback promotes openness in therapy, strengthens the therapeutic alliance, reinforces collaboration, enables any misconceptions about CT to be corrected early in therapy and customizes therapy, within the CT framework, to clients' particular requirements.]

Paul: Well, you've helped me to understand more about my depression and writing it on the board like you did begins to make things clearer.

Therapist: Is there anything I said or did that you weren't too keen on?

Paul: You ask a lot of questions which I can understand why, but things seemed to move a bit too fast at times.

Therapist: Thank you for that feedback. I will slow things down in our next session to a pace that you feel more comfortable with. I look forward to seeing you next week.

Paul: Okay.

Assessment summary

Diagnosis

Paul met the criteria for a major depressive episode whose essential feature 'is a period of at least 2 weeks during which there is either depressed mood or the loss of interest or pleasure in nearly all activities' (American Psychiatric Association (APA), 1994, p. 320). At least four additional items must be included to sustain the diagnosis 'drawn from a list that includes changes in appetite or weight, sleep, and psychomotor activity; decreased energy; feelings of worthlessness or guilt; difficulty thinking, concentrating, or making decisions; or recurrent thoughts of death or suicidal ideation, plans, or attempts' (APA, 1994, p. 320).

Inventory scores

- *Beck Depression Inventory* (BDI): 29 (moderate–severe depression).
- *Hopelessness Scale* (HS) (Beck et al., 1974): 14 (moderate hopelessness). 'Hopelessness, which may be defined as a general set of negative expectancies about oneself and the future, appears to be both a concomitant of depression and a predictor of suicidal behavior' (Reinecke, 1994, p. 70).

Symptom profile

- Cognitive: self-critical, low self-esteem, indecisive, all or nothing thinking, rumination, fleeting suicidal ideas, poor concentration.
- Affective: depression, anxiety, guilt, shame.
- Behavioural: withdrawal from others, inactivity. Other times pacing up and down, crying.
- Motivational: loss of interest and enjoyment, avoidance.
- Physical: apathy, low energy levels.
- Physiological: sleep disturbances, loss of appetite and libido.

Historical perspective

Paul said he had been ambitious for most of his life, beginning at public school when he always strove for high marks in his exams and made sure he got a place in the rugby team. His parents were both high-earning professionals and stressed to their three sons (no daughters) 'that life without success is a life not worth having'. All three sons were constantly encouraged to make their mark and 'not fall back'; the threat of disapproval if 'you did fail seemed to hover in the background'.

Paul was the youngest of three brothers and said he always felt under pressure to emulate their successes (one was a doctor; the other was an architect). Paul said that 'failure' was a dirty word in the house. He spoke of earlier periods in his life when he 'felt down in the dumps but not like I do now', most notably when he got a 2:1 at university rather than the expected first-class degree. This failure drove him even harder: 'If I'm not successful, then what am I?' He had never sought professional help before because 'it wasn't the done thing. Instructions from my parents were to buck my ideas up – "Look at your brothers: they don't feel sorry for themselves when things go wrong". Self-pity was to be despised so I quickly pulled myself together and got on with it. I can't do it this time'.

Case conceptualization (initial)

This tentative conceptualization pulls together past and present information in order to understand why the client has become depressed at this time and uncover the predisposing factors in himself and his life. The conceptualization for Paul took three sessions to accomplish (therapeutic intervention was proceeding at the same time as conceptualization as one procedure does not exclude the practice of the other). A case conceptualization is seen as provisional as further information gleaned from the client and others helps to make it more accurate over time.

Earlier life experiences

Paul remembered that he had a generally happy childhood but during adolescence 'that's when the pressure started to be successful at school, sports whatever'. He took his older brothers' achievements as the benchmark to determine his own success or failure. Parental approval seemed to be contingent on working hard 'so I worked hard to please my parents'.

Core belief(s)

'I'm a failure' (unconditional). This belief was reiterated spontaneously during the course of the initial and subsequent interviews.

Underlying assumptions (conditional)

'These function as guidelines for living, or ground rules for operating in the world, given the truth of the "bottom line" [core belief]' (Fennell, 1997, p. 4). These assumptions can be expressed in a conditional form, often involving an 'if... then' construction:

- 'If I work hard, then I shall be successful and not be rejected by others' (positive assumption).

- 'If I don't measure up, then I shall bring shame on myself and my family because of my failure and be rejected' (negative assumption).

Assumptions can also be stated as rules based on 'should' or 'must' statements:

- 'I should not let others down' (rule).

Strategies to avoid activating core beliefs

Beck (1995, p. 141) suggests that most clients 'operate according to their positive assumptions' and therefore devise behavioural strategies to operationalize these assumptions. These strategies, as long as they are successful, are meant to avoid the activation of negative core beliefs and the emotional distress connected with them:

- Work hard to be successful.
- Keep up with my brothers.
- Keep my parents happy.
- Do what others expect of me.
- Do not dwell on setbacks or feel sorry for myself.

Precipitating factors

These are critical incidents that trigger clients' presenting problems because the behavioural strategies have not been successful at this point in clients' lives. Negative assumptions and core beliefs now activated strongly influence the way clients see and feel about themselves and events in their lives.

Paul's business consultancy failed because 'the contracts dried up'. He said he felt 'devastated' having to make his two colleagues redundant and very anxious about telling his parents and brothers 'the bad news – I'm a failure'.

Personality vulnerability

Even though Paul's depression seemed to have been triggered by the collapse of his business consultancy and therefore might indicate an 'autonomous personality' (emphasis on achievement, freedom and independence), his preoccupation with the feared adverse reactions of significant others (such as disapproval or rejection from his parents) suggested he was more of a 'sociotropic personality' (emphasis on close interpersonal relations and being loved and valued by others) than an autonomous one.

Major emotions

Depression, anxiety, guilt, shame.

Negative automatic thoughts (NATs)

Depressogenic thinking (cognitive theme: loss and devaluation):

- 'It's all gone wrong.'
- 'I'll never recover from this.'
- 'I can't be any good to have let everybody down.'
- 'No one wants to be around a failure.'

Anxiogenic thinking (cognitive theme: danger or threat):

- 'What if I never get any better?'
- 'How can I ever look anybody in the eyes again?'
- 'What's happening to me?'

(Often in anxiety, clients will report their thoughts in the form of questions, which makes their meaning ambiguous or unclear. Turning questions into clear statements is discussed in Chapter 3.)

Guilt-inducing thinking (cognitive theme: moral violation):

- 'I should be caring for my family, not wallowing in self-pity.'
- 'I'm a bad husband and father.'
- 'I shouldn't have let my business fail and put my colleagues out of work.'

Shame-inducing thinking (cognitive theme: public exposure of perceived defect):

- 'I'm weak for being depressed and coming to therapy for help.'
- 'Others will judge me as inferior for not being able to solve my own problems.'

Freeman (1992, p. 19) states that:

> it is essential for the therapist to share the conceptualization ... with the patient so that the patient can know what the therapist is seeing and the direction of the therapy

Also, as part of the collaborative stance of CT, clients may comment on the conceptualization and suggest changes to it. Paul's comments on his case conceptualization are reflected in the following dialogue:

Paul: It seems accurate enough. The bane of my life is this need to be liked, to be approved of. (shaking his head) You know I'm not really that success-driven. I push myself to be successful so that I will please my parents, my brothers, my wife, anybody else who needs to think well of me. It's pathetic. Deep down I don't really care about the failure of the business: it's the reaction of others I really dread. That's why I haven't told my parents or brothers yet.

[Whether Paul's parents or brothers will react in the harsh way that Paul predicts can be put to the test later in therapy. Also, his comments that 'deep down I don't really care about the failure of the business: it's the reactions of others I really dread' provide further evidence that his personality is largely organized around sociotropy rather than autonomy.]

Therapist: What would you like to do about about these key issues of needing others' approval, being successful in order to please them?

Paul: I would like to be more in control of my life, make decisions that please me rather than please others. I don't want to deliberately set out to hurt my parents or others but I want to make up my own mind about my life.

Therapist: We can look at ways of dealing with those issues later in therapy when you are feeling physically and mentally stronger. Is that okay?

Paul: Yes, I would like to do that.

If clients are not interested in or able to explore the case conceptualization at this stage (perhaps the focus is still on struggling to establish a therapeutic alliance) then wait for a more favourable time to present the conceptualization. Blackburn (1996, p. 72) suggests waiting until the seventh or eighth session to present it because:

> by that time the therapist and the patient ha[ve] gathered enough information both in session and in homework assignments to begin to be able to put together the pieces of the jigsaw and get an overall picture.

In this chapter we have discussed the elements of the assessment process in order to arrive at a case conceptualization of clients' presenting problems. In addition, we began the process of socializing clients into CT so as to prepare them for their expected role in therapy. In the next chapter we shall look at eliciting and examining negative automatic thoughts (NATs).

Chapter Three
Eliciting and Examining Negative Automatic Thoughts

We discuss in this chapter how to elicit negative automatic thoughts (NATs) through the use of techniques such as 'guided discovery' and *'in vivo* exposure'. The differences between thoughts and feelings are discussed and NATs are examined and responded to through, among other methods, Socratic questioning and the use of dysfunctional thought records (DTRs).

Automatic thoughts

As discussed in Chapter 1, three levels of cognitions are targeted for examination and change in CT. The most readily accessible is that comprising negative automatic thoughts (NATs); these are usually the first type of cognitions that clients are taught to identify and evaluate. These thoughts usually lie on the fringe of consciousness or just outside it. Often, as Persons (1989, p. 116) says, 'the patient is completely unaware of them; they are so much part of his view of himself and the world that they do not appear distorted or problematic'.

No one is immune from such thoughts and they often 'pop up' when we feel upset. For example, when writing this book the author (MN) might feel angry when he encounters difficulties or blocks and produce a stream of automatic thoughts, such as 'I'll never finish this bloody book! Why the hell do I keep on agreeing to write another book so soon after finishing the last one? You stupid bastard!'. However, these thoughts are transient and after a cup of tea and calm reflection the difficulty is overcome or the block removed. With individuals suffering from prolonged psychological distress, automatic thoughts are difficult to 'turn off', are not submitted to rational reflection or empirical testing, seem plausible to the individual and reflect the content of maladaptive underlying beliefs. Before clients' NATs can be examined and reality-tested, they need to be elicited. A number of techniques for eliciting automatic thoughts are now described.

Guided discovery

This refers to a series of questions asked by therapists to bring information into the awareness of their clients (Beck et al., 1993); this information is the presence of automatic thoughts and their relationship to mood and behaviour. In the following example the client is not sure why he started drinking again:

Client: I remember I was sitting at home on my own listening to some music and the next thing I know I'm down the pub getting pissed.

Therapist: Let's see if we can fill in the gaps between sitting there on your own and getting pissed down the pub. Okay?

Client: Sure. I'd like to know myself.

Therapist: Can you remember how you were feeling or what you were thinking at the time?

Client: Well, you know, the usual stuff like everybody is out enjoying themselves and I'm stuck indoors on my own as usual.

Therapist: So everyone else is out enjoying themselves and you're stuck indoors on your own as usual. Did that seem like a bleak picture to you at the time?

Client: It was very bleak. Like it was never going to end (client stares at the floor).

Therapist: What were you feeling when you thought about this bleak picture of your life?

Client: I felt very angry (client becomes agitated).

Therapist: Can you remember what thoughts or images were going through your mind at that moment to make you feel very angry?

Client: (body posture stiffens) 'Stopping drinking hasn't made me feel any happier. Bloody worse in fact. Fuck everything! I'm going to get slaughtered.'

[The thoughts that propelled the client into drinking again have been uncovered.]

Therapist: So with those thoughts in mind, what happened next?

Client: (slumps in the chair) I got wrecked down the pub. Once I said 'Fuck everything!' that was the point of no return, nothing was going to change my mind.

Therapist: Okay, imagine sitting at home all alone as usual and everybody else is enjoying themselves. What thoughts would you have needed to say to yourself not to have got angry and gone down the pub?

Client: Well, you know, things like 'It won't last forever. Good times will come back again. Drinking is not the answer to my problems'. I wouldn't have felt so bad if I'd thought like that, but I didn't think like that.

Therapist: I know. So what's the point I'm trying to make?

Client: Those thoughts that exploded in my head started me drinking again.

Therapist: Are you still unsure about why you started?

Client: No, everything is clear now. So how do I stop drinking then?

Therapist: We'll come to that.

Through careful questioning, the client is guided to discover for himself why he started drinking again. The client's uncovered NATs are derived from underlying cognitions, which can be revealed and examined later in therapy. A good starting point for this later investigation would be the client's emphatic 'Fuck everything!' which is often a philosophy of despair reflecting core beliefs (for example, 'I'm no good', 'No one cares for me' or 'The world's against me'). Guided discovery is one of the cornerstones of cognitive therapy (Padesky and Greenberger, 1995).

Asking direct questions

This is the most straightforward technique for eliciting NATs: 'What was going through your mind when you felt [specify emotion]?' This form of questioning can quickly establish whether clients have the ability to identify such thoughts. Avoid asking vague, rambling or confusing questions, such as 'What do you think you were thinking about when you were feeling that way that led you to think so negatively in that situation?'. Such questions will bring the investigation for automatic thoughts to a dead stop. Keep your questions short and direct (for example, 'When you were angry, what specific thoughts did you have?' or 'What particular thoughts or images did you have in your mind when you felt anxious?').

In-session emotional changes

Changes in clients' emotional state can occur at any time in therapy and it is important for therapists to be alert to these obvious or subtle affective shifts as they are an important entry point into clients' thinking. For example, a client who is energetically describing a party she went to suddenly sighs deeply:

Therapist: That big sigh seems to indicate that something is going on with you at this very moment. How are you feeling?

Client: I feel very down, very unhappy.

Therapist: What thoughts are going through your mind at this moment?

Client: 'I always go home alone. My friends have no trouble pulling but it's always the same for me. Why doesn't anyone ever want to get off with me?'

The client's question probably implies its own answer but the therapist now seeks to make it explicit. Beck et al. (1979, p. 30) stress the importance of ascertaining meanings in clients' communications:

> the totality of the meaning of the patient's experience is crucial. At times, the meanings people give to a situation may not be fully formulated but rather will have to be drawn out by the therapist ... by relying exclusively on the immediate raw data of the automatic thoughts, the therapist misses the crucial – but unexpressed – meaning.

(for a discussion of the relationship between meaning and emotion, see Beck, 1976). The meaning of the client's last automatic thought is now ascertained:

Therapist: What does that mean about you if no one wants to get off with you?

Client: 'No one thinks I'm attractive and I'll always be on my own' (client starts crying).

The client's reply represents 'hot cognitions'. These are thoughts 'that are most connected to moods ... and conduct the emotional charge' (Greenberger and Padesky, 1995, p. 55) and are usually the most important automatic thoughts to elicit and tackle.

Worst consequences scenario (Wells, 1997)

This involves asking clients, 'What's the worst that could happen if ...

[feared consequences are realized]?'. Padesky and Greenberger (1995) state that this is one of the best questions to ask to identify hot cognitions in anxiety. In this example, a client with performance anxiety is asked to consider the worst:

Client: I'll give a terrible performance.

Therapist: That's a general description of your performance. What specific aspects of it worry you the most?

Client: I'll be so nervous talking to all those people and become tongue-tied.

Therapist: What's the worst that could happen if you become tongue-tied?

Client: I'll just freeze up, nothing will be coming out of my mouth.

Therapist: Is that the worst that could happen?

[The therapist seeks to determine if 'freezing up' itself or its consequences is the worst outcome.]

Client: No. The worst is being exposed as a phoney – people have paid money for the workshop and I can't deliver the goods (the client's key NAT or hottest thought has been identified: 'I'll be exposed as a phoney').

The use of imagery

Uncovering NATS can be a difficult procedure. Without accompanying negative affect related to the situation under discussion, clients can struggle to identify situation-specific hot thoughts (for example, a client is unable to recall what he was so angry about about three weeks ago because he is currently in a relaxed frame of mind in the therapist's office). Weishaar (1993, p. 91) suggests that one reason for this difficulty is

> state-dependent memory: patients are more likely to retrieve memories when they are experiencing the emotions congruent with these memories: for example, negative memories when depressed.

The use of imagery can help clients to recreate past situations in their minds in order to activate the negative feelings and associated automatic thoughts. Ensure that the client describes the situation in the present tense, as if it is happening right now:

Therapist: Now close your eyes and try to remember the sequence of events that occurred in your boss's office three weeks ago when you got very angry. Try to imagine the situation as vividly as you can as if it is happening at this very moment.

Client: Well, he asks me into his office to discuss an important issue. He is on the phone and motions me into a chair. He half-turns his back on me and keeps on talking with no sense of urgency on his part to finish the conversion and talk to me. It's like my time can be wasted by him.

Therapist: How are you feeling at the moment?

Client: I'm feeling irritated with his behaviour but there's more. He takes ten minutes to finish his telephone call, then he spins round in his chair and immediately ticks me off for not pulling my weight on some projects we are working on. He doesn't even ask me for my views on the subject (client is gripping the arms of his chair and his teeth are clenched). He speaks to me like I'm the office junior and then dismisses me. I am so angry with him I could smash a chair over his arrogant head.

Therapist: What does it mean to you to be treated like the office junior and dismissed in this way?

[The therapist's question is intended to draw out more salient automatic thoughts connected to the client's anger.]

Client: That I'm of no importance whatsoever. All my years with the company are meaningless. I am being treated like something he stepped in.

Therapist: Now do you realize what you were so angry about?

Client: Absolutely.

Suggesting thoughts to clients based on your clinical experience

When clients are unable to produce any automatic thoughts because they say, for example, 'Nothing went through my mind at the time', it is usually unproductive to keep on asking variations of the 'What went through your mind?' question as this can increase clients' irritation as they reply with an exasperated, 'I don't know!'. To avoid this outcome, you can suggest to clients, based upon your clinical experience with previous clients who had similar problems to theirs, some of the thoughts they had in order to stimulate recognition:

Therapist: When they became light-headed or dizzy they usually believed they were going to pass out and make a public spectacle of themselves, or they feared the loss of control that fainting would bring, or that no one would come to their aid. Do any of those thoughts ring a bell with you?

Client: Yes, they do ring a bell.

Therapist: Which one or ones in particular ring a bell with you?

[The therapist is seeking evidence that the bell has indeed been rung and the client is not being compliant.]

Client: Losing control worries me.

Therapist: What is it about losing control that worries you?

Client: Well, if I lose control of myself when I panic, then I'm going to pass out and … (long pause) have a stroke. That's what happened to my mother about 30 years ago. That's why I avoid situations where I might panic – I don't want that to happen to me. That connection has only just struck me, isn't that strange.

These 'borrowed' thoughts can stimulate clients to uncover their own idiosyncratic interpretation of their problems and thereby bring into their awareness what was lying outside it.

In vivo exposure

Frequently, anxious clients have difficulty in gaining access to their anxiogenic thinking because they are not in the situations that trigger their anxiety, or they avoid thinking about the situations except in general terms (for example, 'I knew something bad was going to happen so I had to get out of there [or avoid going in the first place]'). In the comparative safety of your office, the 'something bad' remains vague and therefore difficult to pinpoint. By encouraging clients to enter into the feared or avoided situations, hot thoughts can be activated.

For example, a client the author (MN) saw considered himself to be ugly ('I'm sure they call me horseface behind my back' [laughs]). He said his wife kept on at him to take her out for a meal but he was reluctant to sit in a crowded restaurant: 'I'm sure I'm just being silly; there's probably nothing to worry about'. In the therapist's office, we could not 'get at' what lay behind the worry. He agreed to go to a local cafe with me.

Inside the cafe, his anxiety was very evident (he was not laughing now): 'I don't like sitting here with all these people staring at me, scrutinizing me. I know what they are thinking: "Isn't he ugly. Look at the freak". I can't even hold a cup without spilling the tea. I'm shaking like a leaf. It's true: I am a freak. I want to leave now [which we did].' Such exposure to a previously avoided situation yielded crucial assessment data that remained untapped while we were sitting in my office (namely, the hot thoughts or key NATs: 'It's true: I am a freak'). Accompanying your clients on such trips early in therapy is often necessary as they are hardly likely at this stage to carry out such feared tasks alone.

Interoceptive exposure

This refers to exposing clients with panic disorder to bodily sensations that they fear arousing such as breathlessness, palpitations or dizziness. These clients 'have a relatively enduring tendency to interpret certain bodily sensations in a catastrophic fashion' (Clark, 1988, p. 149). From their viewpoint, these sensations, if aroused, will lead to an imminent disaster such as suffocation or insanity. Catastrophic cognitions can be elicited by encouraging clients to engage in interoceptive exposure exercises like running on the spot, spinning in a chair, hyperventilating, staring at bright lights, shaking one's head from side to side (Barlow and Craske, 1989). For example, a client who ran on the spot for two minutes was terrified that 'My heart can't take the strain. My heart will give out in a minute if I don't stop now!' (the client's NATs are revealed through this exercise).

Behavioural assignments

Though the *in vivo* and interoceptive exposure tasks described above are aimed at eliciting hot cognitions usually related to anxiety and panic, behavioural assignments can be carried out with any client problem. (For example, a client said he would get inexplicably sad if he started to clear out the spare room of his past possessions but 'it desperately needs doing'. He agreed to start the task that weekend and record his accompanying cognitions. At the next session he reported his sadness-related automatic thoughts as: 'The best and happiest part of my life is behind me. I only settle for second best now. Why did things turn out badly for me?').

Providing a thought opposite to clients' expected responses (Beck, 1995)

A way of stimulating cognitive awareness with clients who have difficulty specifying automatic thoughts in a particular situation is for you suggest to them the opposite of what might be their hypothesized response:

Therapist: You are anxious about doing the national lottery twice a week. Is that right?

Client: Yes, but I'm not sure why.

Therapist: Are you anxious that you are going to win several million pounds and be very happy for the rest of your life?

Client: Fat chance of that happening. (ponders) No, it's not that. I'm spending more and more money every week on the lottery, scratch cards too.

Therapist: And you're glad spending all this money?

Client: Of course not. I'm not glad at all. I'm becoming a lottery addict and my life will spin out of control because of it (the last sentence finally reveals the client's NATs).

Focusing on emotions

Focusing on feelings can help clients to reveal important automatic thoughts. For example, a client who feels angry with his father's behaviour towards him but is reluctant to tell him, is encouraged to imagine his father sitting in the counselling room and to tell him how he is feeling:

Client: I asked you out for a drink last Sunday and you said you were too busy. You're always too busy. You've got no time for me. I feel you're always pushing me away. What's wrong with me? Tell me!

Therapist: Why do you think he always pushes you away?

[The therapist seeks to pinpoint the client's automatic thoughts.]

Client: 'He doesn't love me. I'm not good enough for him. I'll never be good enough for him no matter what I do.'

The use of chairwork in the above example is usually associated with Gestalt therapy rather than CT. 'CTers' use techniques borrowed from other therapeutic approaches but these borrowed techniques are used in the service of the cognitive model of emotional disorders (Clark and Steer, 1996).

Converting questions into statements

In Paul's case conceptualization in Chapter 2, his anxiogenic thoughts were posed as questions rather than expressed as statements (for example, 'What if I never get any better?'). Even though the implied negative prediction of never getting better seems clear enough, there is still room for ambiguity and potential confusion. Therefore, automatic thoughts in the form of questions cannot be properly examined or adaptive responses developed. In the following dialogue, the therapist helps her client convert questions into statements in order to understand his fears:

Therapist: In cognitive therapy, it is important for both of us to be clear about your thinking – to make it as clear and concrete as possible. So when you say 'What if my wife doesn't love me any more?', do you mean she does or doesn't love you any more?

Client: I mean 'She doesn't love me any longer' (first NAT made explicit).

Therapist: Okay. You also said 'Will I fall apart if she leaves me?' Does this mean that it is more or less likely that you will fall apart if your wife leaves you?

Client: What I mean is 'I will fall apart if she leaves me. I can't cope without her' (second and third NATs made explicit).

Role play

This is used when clients have difficulty uncovering salient cognitions in their problematic relationships with others. The therapist can play the individual with whom the client experiences interpersonal difficulties. It is important for you to take on the characteristics that the client ascribes to the other person if the role play is to have any verisimilitude (for example, if the client says a work colleague is rude and interrupts all the time, do not play him as sweet and charming as this will undermine the role play). Here the therapist plays the role of the client's friend who is always understanding and forgiving and which the client is irritated about:

Client: I'm sorry that I couldn't give you a lift to the station last week. You must have got soaked in all that rain.

Therapist: No problem. A drop of rain never hurt anyone.

Client: Thinking back, I could have given you a lift if I juggled my schedule a little bit.

Therapist: Don't give it a second thought – you did what you thought was right at the time.

Client: (voice rising) Don't you ever get angry about anything?

Therapist: [coming out of role] It seems a nerve has been touched.

Client: I know what it is: he makes me feel guilty.

Therapist: What thoughts are going through your mind now to make you feel guilty?

[The therapist is emphasizing the thought–feeling link and not reinforcing the client's belief that his friend makes him feel guilty.]

Client: That 'I've let him down. I've done something bad. I'm not good enough to be his friend'. What makes it worse is that he always forgives me. I would rather he had a go at me.

Use of the personal voice

Some clients report their thoughts in an impersonal way (for example, 'One would see one's self as a failure in those circumstances', 'Everyone gets nervous if they are going to talk to a large group' and 'We can't help seeing ourselves as fools when things go wrong in our lives, can we'). These thoughts lack a personal voice: what is the client's idiosyncratic interpretation of the situation? Therefore, encourage your clients, or demonstrate it yourself if necessary, to talk in the first person singular (for example, 'I'm a failure' or 'No one likes me'). By this means, clients can claim ownership of their thoughts.

Distinguishing NATs from other, less important, cognitive data

Clients may produce many thoughts about their presenting problems. Some or the majority of these thoughts will be irrelevant or peripheral to clients' current emotional state. It is important that you sift through this cognitive outpouring in order to pinpoint hot (i.e. emotionally charged) thoughts rather than discussing or responding to everything clients say. Confusing situations with NATs can be a common problem. (For example, a client says she got depressed when her boyfriend did not phone her: 'That's why I got depressed. It's not hard to work out, is it?'). What the client actually provides is a situation (her boyfriend not phoning her) and her feelings about this (depression). Crucially, what is missing is her appraisal of the situation which is eventually identified as 'He takes me for granted these days. I mean nothing to him any more. I've lost a wonderful relationship'.

Clients can provide reflections on their thinking rather than the actual thoughts linked to a specific situation. (For example, a client muses on what he may have been anxious about last week during a boardroom meeting: 'Hmm. Let me see. I think I was possibly anxious about not having the exact figures for the chairman. Something like that I think. It all seems so silly now'). These are the opposite of hot thoughts. Through imagery, the boardroom scene is recreated vividly in the here and now and the client's anxious thoughts are revealed as: 'Oh God! I've made a complete and utter fool of myself in front of everyone'.

Clients can often readily produce streams of thoughts connected to their problems but these streams can omit the key thoughts linked to clients' emotional disturbances. For example, a client says she feels guilty about her daughter's behaviour but guilt-inducing thoughts are not evident in the way she communicates her problems:

Client: I do feel guilty about what she's getting up to. You know, staying out late, mixing with bad company, ignoring whatever I say. I wonder what she's up to when she comes in very late. I think to myself: 'Is she on drugs?' That's what I worry about the most. It's always on my mind. Maybe I should confront with her my suspicions. I know she won't like it though. Why does she behave like this?'.

Running parallel with this first stream is a second one containing the NATs or appraisals of the situation. It is important that you help clients to 'tune in' to this second stream in order to locate their emotionally distressing thoughts:

Therapist: Why do you think she behaves like this?

Client: 'I've let her down somewhere. It's my fault she's on drugs. I'm a bad mother for letting this happen to my daughter' (client starts to cry).

[The client's appraisals of the presenting problem have now been uncovered, which then explain her guilt.]

Discovering clients' idiosyncratic meaning of events

'Patients often talk about events as if they were the cause of their bad feelings. The therapist establishes the missing link (the interpretation) by *ascertaining the meaning of the event*' (italics in original; Blackburn and Davidson, 1995, p. 73). A client's view of events might look like this:

Table 3.1: Client's view of events

Event	Feeling
Stuck in a long queue in the supermarket 'which will make me late for the meeting'	Anger

The therapist asks the client what it means to him to be stuck in a long queue in the supermarket which will make him late for the meeting:

Table 3.2: Client's thoughts on event

Event	Thoughts	Feeling
Stuck in a long queue in the supermarket 'which will make me late for the meeting'	My colleagues will think I'm incompetent and lose respect for me	Anger

Thus, the therapist demonstrates to the client that his feelings are mediated by his thoughts about the event and are not directly caused by the event itself.

Analysing a specific incident/situation

When clients talk about their problems in general terms, it can be difficult for therapists to tease out NATs because concrete examples of when the problems are experienced remain elusive. Therefore, it is important to ground the problem in a specific context:

Client: There is no particular time when I worry more. I'm worried all of the time. I'm just a worrier, that's it.

Therapist: It is important for us to pin down some of the worrying thoughts that you have in order for us to begin to understand why you worry all the time. Okay?

Client: Okay, but I can't think of anything.

Therapist: Are you worried at this very moment?

Client: Yes, I am.

Therapist: What specific thoughts are going through your mind at this very moment to make you feel worried?

Client: 'What if I'm wasting my time coming here? What are you going to make me do? I might feel worse after seeing you.'

Instead of seeing worry as an amorphous mass, the therapist isolates and extracts from the client worrying thoughts related to coming to therapy and these then provide a 'way in' to begin to understand the client's subjective experience. Note that the client's first two thoughts are in the form of questions which, as we said earlier, need to be converted into statements (such as, 'I am wasting my time coming here') and then through guided discovery, uncover the implications of wasting time in therapy (for example, 'I'll never be able to stop worrying. No one can help me').

Dysfunctional thought records (DTRs)

DTRs help 'clients learn to distinguish between situations, thoughts and feelings, identify inaccurate thinking, and develop more balanced appraisals' (Tinch and Friedberg, 1996, p. 1; Beck et al., 1979). The DTR comprises a five-column worksheet. In the early stages of therapy, clients are taught to fill in the first three columns in order to gain practice in recognizing, monitoring or 'catching' their automatic thoughts and their links to upsetting feelings (Figure 3.1). Some DTRs put emotions in the second column and thoughts in the third, as clients are usually more able to access their feelings about the situation before their thoughts; other DTRs put thoughts in the second column and emotions in the third to direct clients to the mediational role of their cognitions in their emotional problems. If some clients baulk at the term 'dysfunctional', use the name 'daily thought record' instead.

Identifying emotions and separating them from thoughts

The words 'I feel' are part of everyday usage (for example, 'I feel I work too hard' or 'I feel we should go away this weekend') and no doubt individuals would be startled or annoyed if you corrected them by saying 'When you say "I feel I work too hard" what you really mean is "I think I work too hard"'. You will need to do this tactfully if clients are to understand the distinction between thoughts and feelings in CT, and how the former influence the latter. Greenberger and Padesky (1995, p. 28) suggest emotions 'can be identified in one descriptive word [such as depressed, anxious, angry, guilty, ashamed]. If it takes you more than one word to describe a mood, you may be describing a thought'. For example:

Client: I feel that everything I do is a failure.

Therapist: Okay, you have this thought that everything you do is a failure. Now with that thought in mind, how do you feel – which emotion do you experience?

Client: I feel it shouldn't be happening to me.

Therapist: You've given me a second thought. Feelings can usually be described in one word like anxiety, anger, depression, guilt. With those two thoughts in mind, how do you feel?

Client: Angry!

Some clients may use one word to describe their feelings, such as 'crap', 'bad' or 'horrible'. Unfortunately, these kinds of one-word descriptions, although vivid, do not pinpoint which one-word emotions cognitive therapists are looking for and therefore further investigation is required:

Therapist: When you say you felt bad, I'm not sure which emotion you're referring to. Bad can mean, for example, depressed, ashamed, hurt, angry.

Situation	Automatic thoughts	Emotions	Alternative responses	Outcome
What happened?	What thoughts and/or images are going through your mind right now? Rate belief in thoughts/images 0% – 100%	What emotions are you experiencing? Rate intensity of emotions 0% – 100%	What responses can you make to reply to your automatic thoughts? Rate belief in alternative responses 0% – 100%	Are you thinking and feeling differently? 1. Re-rate belief in automatic thoughts 0% – 100% 2. Re-rate intensity of emotions
My wife asked me to get a few items from the corner shop, but I couldn't be bothered to go. I verbally lashed out at her.	She knows I am not up to it. 80% She's making me feel more helpless. 90% I shouldn't have got angry with my wife. It was wrong. 80% I've let her down for being like this, angry and useless. 100%	Anger. 80% Guilt. 90%		

Figure 3.1: Separating situations, thoughts and feelings; Paul's dysfunctional thought record (DTR).

Client: I'm not sure which feeling it is.

Therapist: Can you tell me more about these bad feelings?

Client: Well, I feel so bad because I slept with my girlfriend's best friend. It would destroy her if she found out. I've behaved so badly towards her. The lies are eating away at me.

Therapist: Your bad feelings sound like guilt. Would that be correct?

Client: Yes. I'm feeling very guilty and I don't know what to do about it.

In the above extract, a distressing emotion has been identified. In order to reduce the client's level of distress, it is the ideas behind the emotion that need to be examined and modified. Emotions are not challenged. As Walen, DiGiuseppe and Dryden (1992, p. 98) state:

> Feelings are not open to dispute; they are phenomenological experiences for which only the individual has data. You cannot argue with such subjective states, whereas thoughts, beliefs, and opinions are open to challenge.

Also, not every negative feeling needs to be addressed (for example, a client expresses disappointment over setbacks in her life but this presents no significant impairment in her everyday functioning). Emotions that are experienced as distressing or disabling are the focus of therapeutic attention.

Making this distinction between thoughts and feelings is necessary but it is also important not to correct clients every time they say 'feel' when they mean 'think' otherwise you may jeopardize the development of the therapeutic relationship ('For heaven's sake, let me finish a sentence without you correcting me all the time'). Obviously, your clinical judgement will guide you when to intervene (such as at a natural pause in clients' communication) and when not to (when a client is very upset).

Eliciting Paul's NATs

Some of these were already elicited during the initial assessment. Paul was familiar with separating his problems into their respective components: situations, automatic thoughts and emotions, through the use of ABC examples seen in Chapter 2. Use of the DTR encourages clients to make explicit their negative thoughts by writing them down, helps them to gain some distance from these thoughts, allows insight into the impact of their thinking on how they are feeling, and provides a between-sessions account of what is going on in clients' lives (though not all clients will feel happy about filling out these forms as they can appear complicated; they can be modified to make them easier to use). In this extract from therapy, Paul is shown how to use the DTR:

Therapist: One way of gaining control over what's happening to you is to start writing things down. I would like to show you this form (passes Paul a DTR) and we can start filling out the first three columns.

Paul: How will filling in this form help me?

Therapist: Instead of your thoughts going round and round in your head, you can learn to pluck some of them out, so to speak, and thereby pin them down for examination. But first you need to start collecting them. So, initially, we are only concerned with the first three columns. Okay?

Paul: Okay. How do we start?

Therapist: Well, it would be better if you fill in the three columns rather than me.

[If your clients are initially reluctant to fill out the forms, you can do it in collaboration with them. Give them a copy of the completed form as a model to follow.]

Paul: All right, if you lend me your pen.

Therapist: Now, column one, can you think of an upsetting situation?

Paul: I feel down most of the time, but I got angry this morning and then I felt guilty.

Therapist: What was the situation? Write it down in the situation column.

Paul: My wife asked me to get a few items from the corner shop, but I couldn't be bothered to go. I verbally lashed out at her.

Therapist: Now you've already identified your feelings as anger and guilt. Write those two feelings down in column three. You'll notice it asks you to rate the intensity of your feelings between 0% and 100%.

Paul: The anger was about 80% and the guilt about 90%.

Therapist: Now we have the situation and the feelings. Column two needs filling in to show how your thoughts about the situation led to your feelings. So what thoughts were going through your mind at that moment?

Paul: I was getting angry because I thought 'She knows I'm not up to it. She's making me feel more helpless'.

Therapist: Now how much did you believe those thoughts at the time – from 0% to 100%?

Paul: The first one about 80% and the second one 90%.

Therapist: Okay, those thoughts are connected to your anger. Now, what thoughts made you feel guilty?

Paul: I thought 'Why did I get angry with my wife?' and . . .

Therapist: Can I interrupt you there? It's important for you to make the contents of your thoughts clear so we can be sure what they actually are. Putting your thoughts in the form of questions can make it difficult to understand the meaning of your thinking. So how would you turn the question into a statement?

Paul: Oh, I see. 'I shouldn't get angry with my wife. It was wrong.'

Therapist: Any other thoughts related to the guilt?

Paul: 'I've let her down for being like this, angry and useless.'

Therapist: How much do you believe these thoughts?

Paul: The first one about 80% and the second 100%.

Therapist: Now would you be prepared to fill out some of these forms in the following week, just the first three columns, in the same way you've done today to gain some practice at collecting these upsetting thoughts?

Paul: Okay. How many do I have to do?

Therapist: I don't want to overload you, so how about three or four of them related to situations you get particularly unhappy about?

Paul: I think I can manage that. What about this form?

Therapist: We can spend the rest of this session answering those thoughts.

Paul: Good.

Examining automatic thoughts

Beck et al. (1979, p. 164) state:

> the therapist's major task is to help the patient think of reasonable responses to his negative cognitions ... to differentiate between a realistic accounting of events and an accounting distorted by idiosyncratic meaning.

By encouraging clients to generate more adaptive responses to their negative thinking, this usually decreases their dysphoria and leads to better problem-solving. In order to achieve this outcome, clients are taught to regard their NATs as hypotheses rather than as facts about themselves, others and the world so they can be reality-tested and evaluated (if a client views an automatic thought as a fact then there is no further evidence to collect and little prospect of developing an alternative perspective).

Examining clients' automatic thoughts is not about you proving your viewpoint is right and your clients' wrong. Examination does not involve challenging, disputing or attacking clients' automatic thoughts. Examination is based on collaborative empiricism to determine the accuracy and helpfulness of clients' thinking. Techniques to examine NATs include the following.

Weighing the evidence

Moorey (1990, p. 20) suggests 'this is probably the most common method of cognitive restructuring'. Clients are taught to weigh the evidence for and against their automatic thoughts (it is important that you do not attempt to manipulate the evidence so as to persuade your clients to arrive at the 'correct' answer). For example, a client who says that a recent workshop she ran was a 'disaster' is asked to go through again the participants' evaluation forms and to concentrate on all the forms and not just the ones that are critical. To her surprise, she finds that the majority of them praised her presentational skills.

Constructing alternative explanations

Based upon the new evidence that the above client has collected, are there alternative explanations that the client can consider regarding the outcome of the workshop? Blackburn and Davidson (1995, p. 76) suggest that by:

> asking the patient to list alternative interpretations of a situation and then *establishing the realistic probability* of each interpretation is a powerful technique, as it does not reject the original negative interpretation, unlikely as it might be, and contrasts it with more likely interpretations. [italics in original]

Following on from the above example:

Therapist: Most of the forms were favourable. What does that suggest to you?

Client: The workshop wasn't a disaster I suppose.

Therapist: When you say 'I suppose' you still seem doubtful.

Client: Well, I got a good response because they were feeling sorry for me.

Therapist: How likely is that?

Client: That's not likely at all. None of them knew me, so why should they do that? There's no reason for them to do that.

Therapist: Any other explanations for getting good evaluations?

Client: Hmm. Could have been a fluke of course, never to happen again.

Therapist: That's possible. Could there be other reasons rather than it was a fluke?

Client: Well, it could be that I will continue to get decent evaluations from other workshops if my presentation remains competent.

Therapist: Any other explanations for the good feedback?

Client: Well, they didn't have to pay to attend the workshop, so they scored me higher than they would have done if they had to pay for it.

Therapist: Do you think that just because they were not paying to attend that they would put up with any standard, no matter how abysmal it was?

Client: (shaking her head) I doubt if they would do that. I certainly wouldn't.

Therapist: Any other explanations for the outcome of the workshop?

Client: Well, the most obvious one is that it wasn't a disaster.

Therapist: If it wasn't a disaster, how would you describe it?

Client: Thinking about it now, it was quite successful after all.

Therapist: Okay. Now let's write these different explanations up on the whiteboard. Your first evaluation of the workshop was that it was a 'disaster'. The evidence from the evaluation forms did not support this conclusion: in fact, most of them were very positive. In the face of this new evidence, you said that the participants were feeling sorry for you, they didn't have to pay, the workshop was a fluke and the workshop was quite successful. Which explanation seems the most plausible in the light of our discussion?

Client: The one that jumps off the board at me is that the workshop was quite successful if I think about it sensibly and realistically.

Therapist: And if you don't think in those ways?

Client: That's when I start seeing everything as a disaster and I get depressed.

The client's alternative explanations for the success of the workshop were still mostly negative and she seemed intent on undermining her own abilities. Clients will often generate alternatives that are as unhelpful or unrealistic as the initial automatic thought, so perseverance is needed to encourage them to come up with evidence-based and more constructive assessments of problematic situations. Also, this client's reluctance to accept that the workshop was a success is probably linked to her underlying beliefs, such as 'Everything that is important to me has to be completely successful'. Such beliefs are uncovered and examined later in therapy when clients have acquired some CT skills in identifying, testing and modifying their NATs.

Advantages and disadvantages

This technique helps clients to tease out the advantages and disadvantages of holding on to a particular thought (for example, 'I should do my best to please everybody') or engaging in a specific behaviour (such as drinking heavily when under pressure). Through discussion of each advantage and disadvantage, clients can learn to revise their attitudes and behaviours and reach a more balanced approach to tackling their problems. Wells (1997, p. 72) states that:

> an effort should be made to generate more disadvantages than advantages ... when the disadvantages of maintaining a behaviour or attitutude outweigh the advantages, the individual should be more motivated to change.

In one of the above examples, the client sees that he gets more problems than solutions through excessive alcohol use and seeks more constructive ways (i.e. non-alcohol based) of coping with pressure. This technique is also known as a 'cost–benefit analysis'.

Identifying cognitive distortions

Chapter 1 listed some of the common cognitive distortions, such as emotional reasoning, that can enter into our thinking when we are distressed. For example, an anxious client says, 'I know that when I walk into a room people are thinking "He's boring. I'm not talking to him."' Clients can be given a list of typical cognitive distortions and asked which ones they can identify in their own thinking (for a fuller list of distortions, see Beck [1995]). In this case the client correctly identified 'mind-reading' as the cognitive distortion at work in his thinking. Such identification and subsequent discussion with the therapist can help clients to correct their cognitive distortions with more accurate appraisals of the situation (for example, 'Realistically, I do not know what people think of me. If I go and talk to them I'll get a better idea. Even if some people do find me boring, that's not evidence of mind-reading but the law of averages – some find me boring, some find me interesting').

Decatastrophizing

Also known as the 'What if...?' technique (Beck and Emery, 1979). Catastrophic thinking envisages the worst possible outcome to our present problems (for example, 'What if I panic in the local supermarket, I shall never be able to get over the shame of behaving like a fool in front of all those people.'). Decatastrophizing involves asking questions such as 'If the worst did occur, would your shame really last for the rest of your life?', 'Is panicking in public really the end of your world?' or 'If people did think you were a fool, could you never disagree with that opinion?' Such questions are not meant to belittle clients' worst fears but to encourage them to re-evaluate these fears in terms of the probability of their occurring and, if realized, accepting and coping constructively with them.

Padesky and Greenberger (1995) suggest that 'What if . . .?' catastrophic thinking (for example, 'What if my partner leaves me and I'm all alone in the world?') can be transformed into 'Then what?' coping strategies (such as 'If that happens then I can learn to be more independent and show myself that living alone does not have to be a frightening experience.').

Reattribution

Clients frequently attribute to themselves sole responsibility or blame for particular events (for example, a mother says she is responsible for her daughter's illicit drug use 'because I went wrong somewhere with her'). Self-blame for causing adverse events is particularly evident with clients experiencing guilt or depression (Dattilio and Freeman, 1992). Reattribution involves clients considering all the possible factors/individuals associated with a particular event and then apportioning a commensurate level of responsibility to those factors/individuals; this technique helps clients to view situations more objectively and thereby reduce their distress. In the above example, the client concludes that peer pressure, the availability of drugs, her daughter's attitudes ('Cannabis is a good drug. It should be legalized'), lifestyle and the boyfriends she goes out with, are more powerful and identifiable determinants of her daughter's current behaviour than the client's belief that she went 'wrong somewhere' during her daughter's upbringing.

Reattribution is not meant to 'let clients off the hook' if they are responsible in some measure for a particular negative outcome, but to encourage them to consider whether they are wholly to blame for it.

Exploring double standards

When clients condemn themselves ('I'm worthless now that I've lost my job') you can ask them if they would apply the same standard to their friends (for example, 'If your best friend lost his job would you condemn him as worthless?'). Clients frequently reply that they would be sympathetic and supportive to their friends. In other words, they have one standard for themselves (harsh and unforgiving) and a different one for others (understanding and compassionate). You can then ask clients, for example: 'If you can treat your friends in this caring way, what prevents you from showing it to yourself?' Also, encourage your clients to consider the effects on their friends if they did condemn them. Once these negative effects have been revealed, clients can usually see the parallels with their own situations.

Decentring

This technique involves helping clients to test the idea that they are the centre of attention. Such clients 'view themselves as being continuously vulnerable to other people's judgements of them. They may feel easily ridiculed, rejected, or suspicious' (Weishaar and Beck, 1986, p. 78). For example, a client who thought that people were staring at her in the street was encouraged to ask a number of them the location of certain roads, shops, the railway station and to ascertain the time in order to determine what other people *actually* were doing. She reported that everyone provided directions or the time for her and '. . . then went about their business without a backward glance at me. Just because I think people are staring at me doesn't make it true as I've proved.' Blackburn and Davidson (1995, p. 78) state that the process of decentring or distancing 'underlies all cognitive modification techniques ... that is the patient is asked to stand away from his thought or interpretation and examine it in a realistic manner'.

Defining terms

This involves asking clients what they mean by the terms they use and thereby exposing any flaws in their thinking (for example, 'What do you mean when you call yourself a failure?'; the client replies that several recent failures in his life mean that he is a failure as a person). Whilst acknowledging failures in clients' lives, such as not passing a driving test or not coming top of the class, therapists may point out to clients that they are making global, negative judgements about themselves based on particular events. In this example, if the client is a failure then logically all he can do is fail; if this belief is reality tested does he actually fail at everything he does, and how will it help his recovery from depression if he continues to condemn himself as a failure?

Gilbert (1992, p. 64) calls this common problem of self-devaluation based on specific failures in one's life the 'IT–ME confusion', i.e. 'I only accept ME if I do IT well. IT–ME confusions often lie behind ideas of worth(lessness) and also self-labelling'. It is more important for your clients to focus on what constructive lessons they can learn from their setbacks instead of engaging in pointless self-condemnation.

The survey method

Burns (1989, p. 107) suggests that:

> one way to evaluate a negative attitude is to ask yourself, 'Would other people agree that this thought is valid?' You can often perform a survey to find out.

A client who felt guilty for letting a friend down ('I'm a lousy friend to her') asked her other friends and work colleagues if her guilt was justified in the circumstances (not being able to lend her friend some money). The client reported that the consensus of opinion was that she was wrong to regard herself as a 'lousy friend' because friendship 'does not mean you have to comply with every request'. The client was greatly relieved to hear this feedback which reduced considerably her guilty feelings. If you use the survey method, ensure that your clients obtain representative samples of opinion and do not just ask individuals who will echo their views.

Turning adversity to advantage

This involves taking a misfortune in one's life and using it to one's ultimate benefit (though it may not be apparant at the time). For example, an individual who was made redundant in his late 40s found it impossible to get a similar job and salary at his age. After months of fruitless effort he decided to 'take the plunge' and eventually became successfully self-employed: 'It's great to be your own boss and make it on your own terms.' Obviously, you will need to be sensitive with this approach as you could be seen by clients as minimizing their adversities while advertising the putative benefits to be derived from them.

Exaggeration and humour

This technique takes clients' ideas to their logical but absurd conclusions in order to develop a more realistic perspective on their problems, for example:

Client: I made a mistake at work. It's the end of everything.

Therapist: (mock seriousness) Oh dear! I expect the company will close down tomorrow, businesses across the country will fail and the whole enconomy will come to a halt.

Client: (laughing) Steady on. It's not as bad as that. You're going over the top.

Therapist: You did say 'It's the end of everything'.

Client: Okay I get the point.

Therapist: Do you agree with it though?

Client: Yes, I do. I'm blowing things way out of proportion.

The use of exaggeration and humour 'may not be a good idea for the patient who is so extremely fragile and vulnerable that he feels ridiculed or criticized by the therapist's humorous or sarcastic remarks' (Persons, 1989, p. 136). Use such techniques with caution, and after a therapeutic relationship has been established.

Behavioural experiments

These are used to test the validity of clients' automatic thoughts and assumptions. They are behavioural techniques used to promote cognitive change. Designing an experiment to test the accuracy of a negative thought provides the opportunity to modify it. For example, a client who considered herself to be very overweight predicted 'that everyone in the swimming pool will look at me and snigger and I won't be able to stay there'. The information collected from the experiment was discussed in the session:

Therapist: What actually happened in the swimming pool?

Client: Well, there were people of all shapes and sizes, so that was a relief.

Therapist: Okay, but what about the specific ideas that everyone in the pool will be looking and sniggering at you and therefore you won't be able to stay there?

Client: Well as far as I could tell, everyone was certainly not looking at me and there was laughter, but of people enjoying themselves, not sniggering at me. I stayed in the pool and had rather a good time.

Therapist: So what lessons have you drawn from this experience?

Client: That what I thought was going to happen didn't occur.

Therapist: So have your ideas weakened or changed?

Client: Oh, definitely weakened. I'm not completely convinced yet.

Therapist: How could you weaken these ideas even further then?

Client: Go swimming once a week. Feel less self-conscious in my swimming costume. I know I'm being silly about all this staring at me stuff, but I think several more visits and I will feel much more relaxed about the whole thing.

Therapist: Sounds good, and we'll review in a few weeks how you got on.

You should not assume that just because a behavioural experiment has proved successful that a more adaptive cognitive response has automatically been generated. It is important that you evaluate the data gained from the experiment and what conclusions the client has drawn from it (the client may have said, for example, that 'if the pool had been less crowded then it would be more likely that people would stare and snigger'). Behavioural experiments form the basis of many homework assignments (see next chapter).

Education

'Information that corrects patients' faulty knowledge or lack of understanding can be used to modify belief in thoughts and schemas [core beliefs]' (Wells, 1997, p. 74; Clark, 1989). To illustrate, catastrophic appraisals associated with symptoms of panic and anxiety (such as dizziness – 'I'm going to faint!', accelerated heart rate – 'I'm having a heart attack!') may be modified with information that these symptoms are harmless (for example, 'I've learned that when I'm anxious my blood pressure rises; in order for me to faint my blood pressure has to drop, so feeling faint does not mean I will faint').

Leaflets, pamphlets, books or short lectures from you can be given to clients as part of their continuing education programme about their psychological disorders and the CT approach to tackling them. When you do present information to clients about their problems ensure that you obtain feedback to determine if and what kind of cognitive restructuring has occurred (for example, 'I know that I probably won't faint now when I panic because of what you explained to me, but you can't guarantee that I won't faint, can you? That's still very troubling to me'). With this example, education cannot provide, nor is it designed to provide, the guarantee the client wants; therefore other techniques would also be used (such as encouraging clients to assume the worst and see themselves coping with it).

Imagery

As discussed in Chapter 1, NATs come in verbal as well as visual form. Some clients find it easier to 'tap into' images rather than thoughts. The use of imagery can help to bring about cognitive modification. For example, a client experienced fearful images of people laughing at him if he made a mistake during a presentation: 'I can see myself crumbling at that point for being so incompetent'; an alternative image that the client developed was to stand patiently and good-humouredly in front of his audience until the laughter subsided: 'It's not the laughter that is the problem but the meaning I attach to it.'

Other imagery techniques include time projection whereby clients are encouraged to look beyond the immediately distressing situation to see that it is time-limited rather than a lifelong state of affairs; and imaginal rehearsal which prepares clients to cope constructively with potentially adverse situations (for example, a former alcoholic imagines himself drinking only orange juice at a party he has been invited to and being assertive with those who are trying to get him to drink alcohol).

Socratic questioning ('guided discovery')

As well as eliciting automatic thoughts, Socratic questioning is also employed to assist clients to 'open up' their thinking in order to develop alternative responses to their problems that may be more helpful or valid than their present thoughts. As Beck et al. (1993, p. 29) observe:

> questioning leads patients to generate options and solutions that they have not considered

and

> this approach puts patients in the 'questioning mode' (as opposed to the 'automatic impulse' mode) so that they will start to evaluate more objectively their various attitudes and beliefs.

Also, through such questioning, clients are enabled to provide their own answers to their NATs rather than accept interpretations that might be offered by therapists.

Padesky (1993a) suggests that guided discovery consists of four steps:

- Questions to reveal information the client is currently unaware of.
- Listening and reflecting by the therapist.
- Summarizing newly acquired information.

- Synthesizing questions so the client can apply the new information to his original belief.

In terms of cognitive restructuring, the last step is the most important one. These four steps will now be demonstrated:

Client: I've been invited to a party this weekend but I'm not sure why I feel anxious about going.

Therapist: When people experience anxiety it's usually because they're worried something unpleasant is going to happen to them.

Client: I'm not sure what it is though.

Therapist: Well, is it that you're going to have a great time and people will not be able to pull themselves away from you?

[The therapist suggests the opposite of a hypothesized fear in order to encourage client introspection – Step 1.]

Client: (shaking his head) Certainly not. I'll be lucky if anybody talks to me.

Therapist: Why would people not want to talk to you at the party?

Client: Because they'll think I'm boring and keep away from me.

Therapist: So is that what you're anxious about if you attend the party?

Client: Yes, that's it.

Therapist: If people do think you're boring, will you agree with them?

Client: Yes, I suppose I will agree with them. It doesn't sound like I'm going to have a good time at the party, does it?

[The client is now aware of what was previously outside his awareness.]

Therapist: Probably not with that thought in mind. (Ponders) There's something I'm not sure about though: if other people think or say you are boring, does that make you boring or can you make up your own mind about this issue?

[The therapist reflects on how the client arrives at labels such as 'boring': is it through accepting others' evaluation of him or through self-evaluation? – Step 2.]

Client: Hmm. I never thought of it like that before. I suppose I do agree too readily if people did consider me boring.

Therapist: And if you didn't agree too readily, but thought carefully about it yourself, what then?

Client: Well, if I really think about it, I've got lots of interests which I find exciting but other people might not. I certainly don't get bored with my life.

Therapist: So it seems you can make up your own mind whether you are boring or not rather than relying on others' opinions of you. You've got lots of exciting interests and you don't get bored with your life.

[The therapist summarizes the new information that has been revealed – Step 3.]

Client: (nods) That's right.

Therapist: So how does this information you've just supplied fit in with your idea that you would agree with other people's opinion of you as boring?

[The therapist asks a synthesizing question which applies the new information to the client's original belief of being boring – Step 4.]

Client: I'm not sure. It doesn't fit in, does it? Maybe I'm not as boring as I think I am.

[However, the client is still endorsing to some extent his negative self-image.]

Therapist: What else could this information point to if you are not as boring as you think you are?

Client: That I could begin to believe I might actually be an interesting person.

Therapist: And how could you believe more in that self-image?

Client: By really making up my own mind about myself and my life. Let others think what they want – I don't have to agree with them as I usually would have done.

Padesky and Greenberger (1995, p. 11) state that such questioning:

> can help a client develop an alternative perspective that the client finds credible because it is based on information provided by the client, not the therapist.

Modelling guided discovery for clients helps them to observe and practise this skill as part of their developing roles as self-therapists.

Writing down alternative responses to negative thoughts

We have described earlier in this chapter that the first three columns of the DTR are used for recording and differentiating between situations, thoughts and feelings. The process of examining NATs results in clients filling in column four with their alternative responses to these thoughts (Figure 3.2).

These responses should be based on the accumulated evidence to date and not on the first thought that enters the client's head, otherwise some of the responses might be unrealistic, overly positive or even more dysfunctional than the original thought being answered:

Therapist: Now the automatic thought is 'He is a complete bastard for running off with someone else'. You said this thought makes you very angry, interferes with your life and you want to stop feeling that way. In what way could you talk back to that thought to help you reduce your anger?

Client: I'm absolutely right: he is a complete bastard. I hate his guts!

Therapist: Will that response help to reduce your anger?

Client: It won't – it'll make my head explode.

Therapist: Shall we try again?

Client: Okay.

Alternative or balanced answers are not meant to be 'perfect' replies, but what Beck et al. (1979) call 'reasonable responses' that will have a beneficial effect on clients' mood and behaviour. If some of your clients are struggling to formulate reasonable responses you might need to provide a few examples for them or 'point them in the right direction'. To return to the dialogue:

Client: I don't really know what to say: he is a bastard.

Therapist: Well, he's physically gone from your life, but mentally he's still there every day and the anger prevents you from getting on with your life and putting him behind you.

Client: I want him completely gone.

Therapist: So what can you say to yourself to start disengaging from him?

Client: 'Calling him names doesn't get me anywhere except angry and it also keeps him in my life. I'm the one that suffers, not him. I've had enough of that so I want it to stop.' I quite like that.

Therapist: Good. We'll see how you can put that into practice.

Situation	Automatic thoughts	Emotions	Alternative responses	Outcome
What happened?	What thoughts and/or images are going through your mind right now? Rate belief in thoughts/images 0% – 100%	What emotions are you experiencing? Rate intensity of emotions 0% – 100%	What responses can you make to reply to your automatic thoughts? Rate belief in alternative responses 0% – 100%	Are you thinking and feeling differently? 1. Re-rate belief in automatic thoughts 0% – 100% 2. Re-rate intensity of emotions
My wife asked me to get a few items from the corner shop, but I couldn't be bothered to go. I verbally lashed out at her.	She knows I am not up to it. 80%	Anger. 80%	I know my wife well enough that she wouldn't ask me if she truly thought I wasn't up to it. She was actually trying to help me. This was confirmed when I asked her. 100%	1. 20% 10% 20% 40% 2. Anger 40% Guilt 50%
	She's making me feel more helpless. 90%		She's not making me feel more helpless. It's just the opposite: she's doing everything she can to help me get better, The less I do the more helpless I feel. That's the real problem. So I'll get over my helplessness by doing more. 100%	
	I shouldn't have got angry with my wife. It was wrong. 80%	Guilt. 90%	I regret getting angry with my wife but it wasn't maliciously intended. I have apologized for my behaviour and explained to her the reasons for it. 80%	
	I've let her down for being like this, angry and useless. 100%		I haven't let my wife or myself down. If I stop calling myself useless, I'll probably spend more time being active around the house. I'll start to see myself as useful instead of useless. 70%	

Figure 3.2: Paul's completed DTR.

Clients are then asked to rate their belief in their new alternative thoughts. Column five asks clients to re-rate their belief in their NATs and reassess the intensity of their associated feelings in the light of these new responses to determine if they have had any positive effect on clients' mood.

Examining Paul's automatic thoughts

After eliciting Paul's automatic thoughts, we now focused on generating adaptive responses to these thoughts to demonstrate to Paul that he was not helpless in the face of his current emotional problems:

Therapist: Now, if we can turn to column four of this form. This looks at answering those thoughts in column two with more accurate and helpful responses. Do you want to continue doing the writing?

Paul: Well, as I've started .

Therapist: Good. Now your first thought is, 'She knows I'm not up to it'. We've gone through some of the ways to respond to these thoughts, what evidence do you have to support that thought?

Paul: There isn't any looking at it now. My wife wouldn't deliberately ask me to do something if she felt I wasn't up to it. I know my wife asked me to go to the corner shop because she thought a breath of fresh air would do me good.

Therapist: How do you know that?

Paul: (Sheepishly) Because I asked her later.

Therapist: So you stopped mind-reading then and checked your wife's actual thoughts. Good. So what response are you going to write down?

Paul: 'I know my wife well enough that she wouldn't ask me if she truly thought I wasn't up to it. She was actually trying to help me. This was confirmed when I asked her.'

Therapist: How much do you believe your response?

Paul: I believe that 100%.

Therapist: The next one is 'She's making me feel more helpless'. Does she have the power to do that?

Paul: That's more nonsense. I feel helpless because of this depression and not being able to see a way out of it. I felt more helpless because I wasn't able to go down to the shop.

Therapist: Can you write down your response then?

Paul: 'She's not making me feel more helpless. It's just the opposite: she's doing everything she can to help me get better. The less I do the more helpless I feel. That's the real problem. So I'll get over my helplessness by doing more.' I believe that 100% too!

[Paul's comment 'I'll get over my helplessness by doing more' will be used by the therapist to suggest to him that some homework tasks should be based on devising daily activity programmes to combat his feelings of helplessness.]

Therapist: Okay. Those are the thoughts connected to your anger. Let's look at the ones connected to your guilt. First: 'I shouldn't have got angry with my wife. It was wrong.'

Paul: Hmm. I'm not sure about that one. I did get angry with her. I can't just brush it under the carpet.

Therapist: I'm not asking you to brush it under the carpet. Did you get angry with her to try and hurt her, was it intended maliciously?

Paul: Of course not. I would never do anything to hurt her intentionally. I love my wife. I regret what I did. I have apologized to her.

Therapist: Okay, write down your next response.

Paul: 'I regret getting angry with my wife, but it wasn't intended maliciously. I have apologized for my behaviour and explained to her the reasons for it.' I believe that 80%.

Therapist: The last thought was 'I've let her down for being like this, angry and useless'. This thought you believed the most.

Paul: That's right.

Therapist: If you have let her down, how do you think she would be behaving?

Paul: Keeping her distance, not talking to me, that sort of thing.

Therapist: Is that happening?

Paul: No. She's very supportive.

Therapist: So in what way in your mind have you let her down?

Paul: By being depressed.

Therapist: So by having an illness like depression you've let her down. If your wife said she had let you down by being depressed, what would you say to her?

Paul: That would be ridiculous, wouldn't it? She couldn't help being depressed. The important thing would be for her to get better as soon as possible.

Therapist: So what prevents you from applying the same understanding to yourself?

Paul: I don't know. I just feel useless.

Therapist: Just because you feel something doesn't make it necessarily true. Feelings are not facts, so let's consider some facts. If you were 'useless', what would you be like?

Paul: I'd never leave the armchair, just sit there all day staring at the wall.

Therapist: So how did you manage to leave your armchair to get here?

Paul: I forced myself out of it.

Therapist: What's your purpose in coming here?

Paul: I don't want to be depressed. I want to get my life moving again, get better.

Therapist: So how do your efforts (emphasizes word) to get better square with your view of yourself as useless?

Paul: It doesn't square with the facts. (Smiles) Maybe I'm not useless after all.

Therapist: If you stop calling yourself 'useless', what benefits would you get from that?

Paul: I'd do more around the house and probably be less of a burden to everyone.

Therapist: So what will you write down to answer this last thought that you've let your wife down for being this way, angry and useless?

Paul: I've already dealt with being angry at her. I'll write 'I haven't let my wife or myself down. If I stop calling myself "useless", I'll probably spend more time being active around the house. I'll start to see myself as useful instead of useless'. I'll give that 70%.

Therapist: Can you see the value of doing this exercise?

Paul: You're getting me to think more carefully about my thinking as if it can't be trusted while I'm depressed.

Therapist: When a person becomes depressed, his thinking usually becomes distorted and turned against himself (client nods); so it is important to help him to consider carefully all the available evidence before drawing conclusions, making judgements. In this way, he can learn to make more accurate assessments of his current situation, which can then help to improve how he feels.

Paul: I'm feeling better at the moment, so I can see how it works.

For reasons of space, not all the dialogue between the therapist (MN) and Paul has been included, thereby giving the impression that generating adaptive responses is straightforward or even simplistic. This is not the case. This procedure can be very difficult, particularly when clients 'shoot down' any attempts at generating reasonable responses (for example, 'Nothing will convince me that I shouldn't have made that mistake'). Obviously your patience will be tested with these clients, but it is important that the therapeutic relationship does not become a battle of wills, as this means winners and losers. Ultimately, some suggestion, observation or question from you can provide the pathway to a response that the client finally finds credible.

The final column on Paul's DTR was completed (i.e. re-rating his belief in his automatic thoughts and reassessing the intensity of his feelings). As clients gain competence and confidence in filling out these forms, they usually find the process of identifying, examining and responding to their automatic thoughts quickens, thereby allowing them to carry out this process mentally. The thought forms can always remain on standby if clients need to 'return to basics' from time to time. The work that is done in the sessions needs to be integrated into the everyday lives of clients; this is achieved through carrying out homework, the subject of the next chapter.

Chapter Four
Homework

In this chapter we discuss, among other things, the importance of homework tasks; types of homework tasks; that homework should logically follow on from the session work and be related to clients' goals; troubleshooting obstacles to homework completion and reviewing assignments at the next session.

The importance of homework

If clients spend only one hour per week in therapy with you what are they going to do with the other 167 hours before their next appointment? Homework assignments provide opportunities for clients to practise in real life the CT skills they have learned in your office. As Persons (1989, p. 141) observes:

> No matter how many insights and changes occur during the session, patients will not solve the problems on their problem list or make significant changes in their underlying irrational beliefs unless they make behavioral and cognitive changes outside the session.

Clients often say how they believe intellectually, but not emotionally, their adaptive responses to their negative thinking. This division between intellectual and emotional insight hinges on clients' degree of belief or conviction in these responses. (For example, a client says 'I know intellectually that there is nothing wrong in being single as it will help me to be self-reliant and enjoy my own company but emotionally I don't feel it's true – I do need a partner to be happy.') In order to test this 'emotional' viewpoint, the client agrees to remain single for several months. This enables her to strengthen her conviction in her new ideas (i.e. believe them emotionally as well as intellectually) as she acts against the old dysfunctional beliefs and in support of her new adaptive beliefs.

Beck et al. (1979, p. 272) state that 'the patient is encouraged to view homework as an *integral, vital component* of treatment. Homework is not just an elective, adjunct procedure' [italics in original]. Therefore clients should be encouraged to carry out homework tasks from the first session onwards rather than delay implementation of these tasks until they feel more comfortable with the CT format. Homework tasks are discussed and agreed collaboratively but in the early stages of CT, therapists usually take a more active role in setting such tasks.

Homework tasks allow clients to develop confidence and competence in tackling their problems, thereby reducing the chances of a full-blown relapse; in addition, clients are less likely to become dependent on you as the agent of change in their lives (imagine clients putting their lives on hold between sessions because the session itself is seen as the crucible of change, not what happens outside it). The ultimate goal of CT is for clients to become their own therapists or problem-solvers; homework facilitates and accelerates progress towards this goal as well as reduces the time clients spend in therapy. Research indicates that clients who carry out homework tasks make better progress than those who do not (Maultsby, 1971; Persons, Burns and Perloff, 1988; Neimeyer and Feixas, 1990; Burns and Nolen-Hoeksema, 1991; Burns and Auerbach, 1992). You can point this out to clients who drag their feet over executing homework tasks.

Types of homework tasks

These may be listed as 'cognitive' (including imagery), 'behavioural' and 'emotive' and are used to modify maladaptive thinking.

Cognitive assignments

Bibliotherapy

These are reading assignments which not only help clients to understand better their psychological disorders but also the CT methods for tackling them. There is a substantial body of CT self-help literature you can recommend to your clients (for example, *Feeling Good* by David Burns (1980), *Love is Never Enough* by Aaron Beck (1988), *Manage Your Mind* by Gillian Butler and Tony Hope (1995), *Overcoming Anxiety* by Helen Kennerley (1997), *Overcoming Depression* by Paul Gilbert (1997) and *Overcoming Traumatic Stress* by Claudia Herbert and Ann Wetmore (1999)). Self-help literature does not by itself help clients to overcome their problems but acts as a useful educational adjunct to therapy. You should acquaint yourself with this literature if you want to suggest relevant reading material as homework. Always ascertain if your clients have any reading difficulties and/or their level of interest in such assignments. As with all homework tasks, ensure that you obtain client feedback on what they have read.

Listening

Clients are encouraged to tape-record each session in order for them to reflect upon its content away from your office; some clients may listen several times to each session, thereby greatly enhancing its effect upon them. Listening to these tapes between sessions often engenders greater understanding of important therapeutic points made in the sessions. Some clients may process information inadequately during therapy with you because they are emotionally disturbed or they may be reluctant to admit they do not understand the points you are making. On their own, they are likely to feel less inhibited or distracted and thereby more able to focus on the session tape.

If some clients develop adverse reactions to hearing themselves on tape ('I hate sounding so negative all the time'), these reactions can be explored and answered at the next session (for example, 'My response to the tape is another example of me being negative but provides more information about my problems. If I learn to listen to the tapes without being so self-critical, I will be able to make faster progress'). Some clients may become insistent that taping should stop, then comply with their requests.

Writing

Filling in DTRs or variations of them are the main writing activities clients engage in; these forms help them to record and respond to their NATs and disturbed feelings with greater objectivity. When clients progress to working at deeper cognitive levels, they can use different forms to modify their dysfunctional underlying assumptions and core beliefs (see Chapter 5). Writing assignments can encompass any project that will help clients to understand and tackle their problems more effectively. (For example, a client agreed to write an essay on what the rest of her life would be like if she kept going out with men who treated her badly.)

Imagery assignments

Coping imagery

A client who predicts that he will forget what he is talking about 'and look like a dummy in front of those GPs' is encouraged to change the ending by imagining himself asking someone in the audience 'What was I just saying?' as a prompt to get his train of thought back on track. Such imaginal problem-solving helps to raise the client's level of self-efficacy and thereby weaken his view of himself as a 'dummy'. The client can then practise this new coping image before undertaking the actual presentation to the GPs.

Inaction versus action imagery

Clients who are poorly motivated to engage in problem-solving can be encouraged to do so through this imagery exercise (Neenan and Palmer, 1998). Clients are asked to imagine as graphically as possible the consequences of not dealing with their fear of failure (for example, never going after what they want from life, endless procrastination) and then contrasting this bleak picture with action imagery (such as taking risks in order to create greater opportunities for themselves, 'doing' instead of 'stewing'). Clients may then carry out this imagery exercise on a daily basis for the next few weeks and then gradually fade out the inaction imagery.

Behavioural assignments

Activity scheduling

This technique is frequently used with depressed clients to increase activity levels and motivation and reduce indecisiveness and excessive rumination on negative thoughts by structuring their days with a series of agreed activities. The day is divided up usually into hourly time periods (such as 9 am to 10 am; 10 am to 11 am) and is planned in advance so clients do not have to decide every hour what to do next. These activities also ask clients to rate on a scale from 0 to 10 how much pleasure and sense of mastery they gained from each task. This helps clients to test their predictions that they will not accomplish any activity or get pleasure from it.

Graded task assignments

These help clients to tackle their problems with small, manageable steps and then progress to tasks of increasing difficulty. For example, a client who said that 'I'm not able to clean my house at all' agreed to undertake small cleaning assignments, such as washing a few cups and saucers, dusting the television, then feedback about these tasks was elicited e.g. 'I suppose I was able to do more than I thought'. Pleased with these accomplishments, homework tasks involved more difficult assignments (such as cleaning a whole room). Each task is based on what can be realistically achieved at any given time rather than on the unrealistic goals clients often set for themselves (for example, 'I should be able to clean the whole house every day even if I don't feel like it').

Behavioural experiments

These were discussed in the previous chapter. To add to that discussion, plentiful opportunities are usually provided by clients' problems to test their thoughts and beliefs. Carrying out experiments allows clients to develop the role of personal scientist whereby their cognitions are treated as hypotheses and then tested empirically; the resulting data are discussed, conclusions are drawn and compared with clients' original hypotheses (i.e. negative predictions). Of course, if an experiment has turned out successfully, clients can still attempt to undermine the conclusions (for example, 'So what? Just because someone returned a phone call, is that supposed to prove that I do have friends?'). In this case, more experiments will need to be designed to test whether the client does have friends, as he remains presently unconvinced. Such experiments help to accumulate evidence that contradicts clients' negative thinking.

If the experiment was unsuccessful (i.e. the client's phone call was not returned), you may ask if there are other interpretations apart from his being friendless. Could his friend have been busy or arrived home very late? What was the message left on the friend's answerphone and in what tone of voice? Did the client go out that evening and miss the phone call? Answers to such questions can help the client to decide if the experiment should be repeated or modified in some way or if it was 'tampered with' (for example, the client reveals that he left a garbled message on his friend's answerphone).

Emotive techniques

Identifying emotions

Some clients may have difficulties in identifying their feelings apart from catch-all descriptions such as 'bad', 'stressed' or 'tired'. As discussed in Chapter 3, emotions can be described in one word, such as 'angry', 'depressed', 'hurt', 'jealous', 'guilty', 'anxious' or 'ashamed'. If clients lack an affective vocabulary, you can produce one as a guide for them to follow. Ways to identify emotions include noticing:

> changes in your body tension. Tight shoulders may signal that you are afraid or tense; a heaviness throughout your body may signal depression or disappointment and see if you can notice three different moods a day (Greenberger and Padesky, 1995, p. 27).

Clients can keep a diary in order to identify their feelings, learn to differentiate between affective states (for example shame and guilt; depression and sadness) and rate the intensity (0–10%) of their feelings; this enables them to decide which emotions are to be targeted for change (for example, a client pinpoints anger and hurt as the disabling and intense emotions she wants to discuss as a result of tracking her feelings for a week). By becoming more aware of their emotions, clients can learn to stand back from them and focus on the dysfunctional thinking connected to excessive emotional reactions to life events.

Building emotional tolerance

This starts in-session by evoking clients' painful or uncomfortable feelings which they usually avoid experiencing. For example, if a client reports that 'I couldn't bear talking about I how feel', you can encourage the client to 'stay with' her feelings in order to elicit accompanying hot (i.e. emotionally charged) thoughts as well as help her to contradict her belief that she could not bear to talk about these feelings. As tolerance builds, clients can construct hierarchies of increasingly painful topics for in-session discussion.

For homework, 'patients can also construct hierarchies for assignments outside of therapy to increase tolerance for negative emotions. Such assignments can be labeled "dysphoria practice" or "antiavoidance activities"' (Beck et al., 1990, p. 271). Such assignments may involve engaging in a boring activity for 45 minutes or thinking at length about a past rejection that the client is still upset about. Clients can compare their predictions about carrying out these tasks ('If I think about him dumping me, I'll collapse into uncontrollable crying') with what actually happened in order to provide further evidence that they can tolerate painful affect.

Anti-shame exercises :

When individuals experience shame, they imagine that others will judge them as inferior, foolish, weak or different in some way because of their perceived flaws or defects and thereby they will lose their approval. For example, a client avoids writing in front of others because of his dyslexia; he fears that if others do see his poor spelling, they will call him an 'idiot' – an evaluation he would agree with. An anti-shame exercise for such a client would be for him to write in public, exposing his poor spelling but not choosing any longer to agree with others' actual or imagined name-calling of him because he now refrains from putting himself down because of his dyslexia. Thus 'if he pursues this "open policy" long enough, his proneness to experience counterproductive shame will diminish' (Beck et al., 1979, p. 179).

Providing a rationale for homework

The importance of homework was discussed at the beginning of this chapter, and this importance should be clearly communicated to your clients. In essence, if they do not put into daily practice what they have learned in therapy little, if any, lasting progress is likely to be achieved. Providing a rationale for homework usually operates at two levels: first, for the general principle and practice of homework and, second, for every assignment that is to be carried out (some clients can quickly forget why homework is crucial for therapeutic change). If you or your client dislike the word 'homework' substitute a more palatable term.

Collaborative homework setting

Obvious as it may seem, collaboration is about working together. In our experience, therapists can fall into the trap of telling clients what their homework tasks should be for some of the following reasons:

- 'The therapist knows best.'
- Clients are too slow or hesitant in making up their minds about what to do.
- Therapists want their clients 'to feel good about themselves' as quickly as possible.
- Therapists' goals for change are more ambitious than their clients'.
- Therapists have to prove their clinical competence by forcing the pace of change.

Padesky and Greenberger (1995, p. 25) advise therapists not to 'ask clients to do things they are not willing to do or that you would not do yourself'.

Telling clients what their assignments will be often leads to understandable resistance or arguing on their part, or compliance in your office but non-compliance outside. If you monitor clients' non-verbal reactions (such as jaw tightening, eye-rolling, staring into the distance) and/or paraverbal responses (a few grunts; a string of 'hmms'), these will usually indicate whether your clients agree with your suggestions. Collaborative homework setting is demonstrated in the following dialogue:

Therapist: We've been discussing in this session your avoidance of making a decision about a career change because you might make the wrong decision, and all the problems that will result from this. On the other hand, you're becoming increasingly frustrated with yourself because you won't make the decision (client nods). So what would be the first step in breaking this deadlock?

Client: I'm not sure about that also.

Therapist: Okay. Do you want to postpone making any kind of decision for several more weeks?

Client: No. I need to do something now but I don't know what.

Therapist: Do you want to make the decision about the career change in the next week?

Client: No, that's much too soon. I need to get going on something though, but I'm stuck for answers. What would you suggest?

Therapist: I would suggest, as a first step, listing the advantages and disadvantages of not making a decision and then doing the same thing for making a decision.

Client: That sounds reasonable and not too frightening. I can't see the harm in that.

Therapist: In what way do you think this task will help you?

Client: I think it will begin to free me from this paralysis I'm in and get the decision-making process rolling.

Therapist: So are we agreed on the homework task for the next week?

Client: We are.

Therapist: Okay, let me make a note of the task and give you a copy of it.

[Giving clients a copy of the homework task greatly reduces the potential disagreements at the next session over what the task actually was.]

When collaborating on homework assignments, the general rule is 'the simpler the better' (Wills and Sanders, 1997). It is better that clients do something, no matter how small, than nothing at all. If some clients do not feel 'stretched' by the assignments, they can always bring this to your attention.

'Win–win' formula of homework tasks

This means that whatever happens with homework tasks, important information will be obtained (everything that happens in or out of therapy is grist to the cognitive mill). Thus, if the client carries out the agreed task, how was this accomplished? If the client carries out a task but not the agreed one, what happened to alter the task? If the task is not attempted, what prevented the client from carrying it out? With regard to the last question, Beck et al. (1979, pp. 276–277) state that:

the therapist should be alert to identify and correct the patient's conclusion that homework which was attempted but not completed represents a failure. Rather, *any* attempt at a new task is a success in its own right. Data which patients report about incomplete assignments often are as useful as a completed assignment.

If you state in advance to clients what the outcome of the homework tasks should be, anything that falls short of this outcome may be dismissed by them as 'not good enough' and thereby create greater reluctance on their part to undertake further tasks. A learning experience can be gained from whatever happens with homework and it is your task to help the client uncover this learning:

Client: I didn't do the homework. I kept on telling myself every day to do it but nothing happened. I just couldn't be bothered.

Therapist: What did you actually say to yourself?

Client: 'Get off your arse and do the work you lazy cow. Stop lying around feeling sorry for yourself. You're pathetic!'

Therapist: Were those thoughts supposed to be words of encouragement?

Client: Well, sort of. If I give myself a hard time, then I'll start sorting my life out. That's the theory anyway.

Therapist: Is it working in practice so far?

Client: No.

Therapist: So why do you have to be so hard on yourself?

Client: Well, because of all those wasted years on drink and drugs.

Therapist: So if you punish yourself for those wasted years through name-calling, then this will motivate you to build a drug-free life. Is that right? (client nods) What do you think will be the consequences of pursuing this strategy?

Client: It's going to backfire. I know it will.

Therapist: Because . . .?

Client: I gave myself a hard time before and that's one of the reasons I kept on getting drunk or stoned.

Therapist: Based on the evidence, that kind of strategy doesn't work. So what is more likely to work then?

Client: Being kinder to myself but I'm not sure how to do that?

Therapist: Let's see if we can come up with something. What words of encouragement will help you to be bothered and carry out some homework tasks?

Client: Well, something like 'I don't want to be different any more. I just want to be like everyone else, getting on with things'.

Therapist: Do you want to write that down on a piece of white card and carry it with you?

Client: Okay. How will that help me?

Therapist: How do you think it will help you?

Client: Well, I guess it will help to remind me of what I'm aiming for in my life and therefore should encourage me. Do you think it will work?

Therapist: Let's put it to the test and review what happened in the next session. Okay?

Client: That sounds fair.

Even though we describe homework as a 'win–win' formula, in reality, if some clients make only half-hearted attempts to or never execute homework tasks, little progress will be made. This is an important point for your clients to understand.

Use of the case conceptualization to design effective homework tasks (Persons, 1989)

When trying to decide what tasks would be therapeutically potent for each client, the case conceptualization provides a guide in this respect. For example, the therapist (MN) saw a client who went from one disastrous relationship to another and became increasingly depressed over each rejection. Some of her automatic thoughts were 'I can't cope on my own' and 'I can't be happy without a partner'. These thoughts were derived from her underlying belief: 'If I haven't got a man in my life then I'm nothing'. The client's solution to her problems was to find another man as quickly as possible and homework tasks should be directed towards this end. If the therapist had agreed with her wishes, therapy would have reinforced her problems rather than ameliorated them. As Persons (1989, p. 144) observes:

> the homework assignment is a helpful one if it involves an activity that works to provide some evidence against the patient's automatic thoughts and central underlying beliefs. If the activity is consistent with the underlying beliefs, it will strengthen those beliefs, and therefore is counter-therapeutic.

If the therapist had gone along with the client's solution, she would have left therapy even more convinced that she was nothing without a man in her life. After much discussion, she decided to keep away from men for an initial period of six months and homework tasks were based on building a more enjoyable and independent life, thereby developing a new self-image and weakening the old one. Eventually, following this strategy, she was able to choose partners on the basis of genuine desire instead of desperation and loneliness.

Is the task relevant to what was discussed or done in the session?

Homework tasks should flow naturally from the work carried out in the session. For example, if you have emphasized the importance of behavioural activities then do not negotiate a cognitive one, such as reading; if you have been discussing an exposure programme then do not suggest engaging in distraction methods. You should ask yourself: 'Is this task the logical outcome of the session work?' If your clients cannot see, explain or agree with the session work– homework–goal link you have suggested, then think again about the relevance of the proposed assignment.

Padesky and Greenberger (1995) suggest that as well as assignments being related to clients' goals, they should also be 'as interesting as possible'. We have often witnessed students suggesting homework tasks that fail to interest clients, let alone fire their imaginations. You may need to suggest several assignments to clients and ask them to rate these tasks in terms of interest. For example, 'Based upon what we did in today's session regarding your anxiety at work, do you want to remain quiet in the meeting until you feel more confident, speak up after the others, or even speak up first?' The client chooses the last suggestion as the most interesting as 'it's both scary and exciting at the same time'.

Even though clients have agreed to carry out the tasks, do they have sufficient skills to make task-completion more likely? (For example, if a client has a problem of unassertiveness with her partner then it is highly unlikely that she will suddenly stand up for herself.) Examining the blocks to unassertiveness ('He might leave me if I start telling him what I want for a change', 'I can't bear it when he's angry') and in-session rehearsal of assertive behaviour would be required before clients feel ready to stand up for themselves. Therefore, skills assessment is another task you need to undertake as part of homework setting.

When, where and how often?

When clients say, for example, 'Yeah, I'll get round to the homework in a few days' this usually means they will not carry out the negotiated task or it is not a priority for them, to be 'fitted in' if they remember to do it and if nothing more interesting intervenes. In order to concentrate clients' minds on carrying out their agreed tasks, ask them the following questions:

- When will you carry out the task?
- Where will you do it?
- How often will you do it?

Specificity, not vagueness, should guide collaborative homework setting and thereby make it more likely that clients will commit themselves to executing their assignments.

Starting homework in the session (Beck, 1995)

During the early stages of therapy, starting homework in the session provides the fillip for clients to continue it outside the session. Beck (1995, p. 256) observes that:

> patients often describe the hardest part of doing homework as the period *just before* they start it – that is, motivating themselves to get started [italics in original].

For example, one of the authors (MN) saw a client who was procrastinating over writing a college essay; she agreed to start it in the session, which then created the momentum to continue it at home. Blocks to writing the essay were identified ('I have to finish it at one sitting without any mistakes') and tackled (the client agreed to divide the essay into stages and write each one in rough draft; revising them would come later). Writing assignments, imagery exercises or practising new behaviours can begin before the end of the session and any problems in executing them can be addressed.

Rewards and penalties

These can be used as further encouragement for clients to carry out their homework tasks. Rewards can be anything that clients enjoy and are not harmful to them or others and do not exacerbate their existing problems (for example, a binge eater should not gorge herself on cakes as a reward). Clients reward themselves *after* they have carried out their assignments, and penalties (not punishments) are self-administered for not carrying them out (for example, watching a boring television programme for 30 minutes).

However, the principle of rewards and penalties should be treated with caution as it:

> can usually only be used with highly motivated clients. If your client seems to be struggling with just getting to therapy sessions, let alone completing assign-

ments outside of therapy, then this intervention may not be appropriate for her. In fact, it may just contribute to an overall sense of failure if used with certain clients (Ellis and MacLaren, 1998, p. 93).

Troubleshooting obstacles to undertaking homework assignments

Once clients have understood and agreed with the rationale for carrying out their homework task and have stated when, where and how often they are going to do them, the next step is to discuss any potential or actual blocks to homework completion. Not only are blocks identified but methods for overcoming them are also discussed. For example:

Therapist: You've agreed to get up every morning at the same time for the next week, whether or not you've had a good night's sleep, as part of your sleep improvement programme.

Client: Yes.

Therapist: Can you see any difficulties or obstacles to carrying out this programme?

Client: Well, the big one will actually be getting up if I've had only a couple of hours' sleep.

Therapist: What thoughts will pop into your head to keep you in bed?

Client: 'This is stupid getting up now. I haven't had a decent night's sleep. I'm not walking round like a bloody zombie!'

Therapist: What will be the consequences if you do sleep in?

Client: It will definitely mess up my next night's sleep. I know it's a vicious circle. It's going to be difficult though answering my automatic thoughts when the alarm goes off.

Therapist: Can you think of anything that will help you to answer these thoughts?

Client: Well, I guess I could place a big sign next to the alarm clock saying: 'Get up'.

Therapist: How about adding 'and get moving!'?

Client: Why do I need that bit?

Therapist: What will happen if you get up and then flop straight into an armchair?

Client: I'll doze off. Point taken. It won't just take a week to get my normal sleep pattern back, will it?

Therapist: No, not after all the years you've been on sleeping tablets. This is just the first step along with other sleep improvement measures we've discussed. Any other obstacles to carrying out the task?

Client: What happens if it doesn't work?

Therapist: Well we won't know either way until the programme gets going, then we can see what's happening and make adjustments to the programme if necessary. What will be the results if you don't carry out the programme?

Client: I won't make any progress on my sleep, that's for sure. I certainly don't want that. I suppose it's a question of 'nothing ventured, nothing gained'.

Therapist: You could write that down on your card as well to remind you of the potential gains to be had.

Client: Okay.

Therapist: Any other obstacles you can think of?

Client: No, that's it for the time being. Okay, I'll give this programme a try then.

If clients are unable to identify any blocks to homework completion, you can suggest some on the basis of your clinical experience (for example, 'Clients often say they will have difficulty in finding the time to do these tasks or will forget to do them; will you have any of these difficulties?'). Homework will often trigger underlying beliefs that hinder task-completion. A common one is the amount of work that clients will have to engage in if progress is to be made, such as 'If it's too hard work overcoming my problems, I won't do it'. Although it is important to point out to clients that sustained effort equals therapeutic change (such as gradually dropping safety behaviours in tackling panic), they can also undertake homework tasks that involve minimal or no effort to determine if change can occur in this fashion. Clients usually see that the 'homework is to do no homework' strategy is a self-defeating one.

Difficulties in executing homework tasks can be predicted based upon clients' case conceptualizations, i.e. obstacles to homework completion are often related to clients' presenting problems (procrastination, perfectionism). One of the authors (MN) once saw a perfectionistic client whose key belief was 'I must do important things perfectly otherwise I'm a complete failure'. This belief determined his discussion of homework: he insisted on a one-off super-duper homework task that would immediately and fully resolve his problems: 'The task is to sit down and write the article in one go, no matter how long it takes – there's the solution' he concluded. The client was impervious to any other suggestions and therefore homework was seen by him as the solution and by the author as an experiment. Even though the client's decision was unlikely to be successful, the reasons for making it could be examined and the outcome of the decision evaluated at the next session.

The client did not even start the task, which reinforced his self-image as a failure and deepened his depression. After much discussion, he finally agreed to break down his assignments into small, manageable steps following Hauck's (1982, p. 47) assertion that:

> *it is more important to do than to do well* ... think of success rather as a slight bit of improvement over what you were able to do before. Even if you are trying something and do not see improvement, you are still entitled to say that you are improving, because the benefits of practice will show up later [italics in original].

Eventually, the client was able to see success as involving both progress and setbacks instead of as an all-or-nothing experience.

The non-linear model of change

Following on from the comments in the last sentence, it is important to point out to clients that change does not mean the eradication of their problems but, rather, they have become more manageable and therefore less disruptive in their lives. By this yardstick, change is viewed in 'relative' rather than 'absolute' terms (for example, clients who have been abstinent from drug use may experience relapses but this does not erase the time they were 'clean'; relapses are seen as part of the recovery process). Change can be measured along the following three dimensions:

- Frequency – is the problem experienced less frequently than before?
- Intensity – is the problem less intense than before?
- Duration – does the problem last for shorter periods?

Clients can become disillusioned because of their perceived lack of progress when, for example, change is much harder than they expected ('Nothing is going right at all'). By setting clearly defined goals at the outset of therapy, clients may be reminded of them as benchmarks of progress: 'One of your goals was to be able to go shopping in the high street on your own. When I first met you, you were housebound. At the moment, you can get to the corner shop on your own. In what way does this represent no progress on your part?' Such reminders can help to combat clients' pessimism about their apparent lack of progress and thereby motivate them to remain in therapy.

Do not rush homework setting

It is hoped that this chapter makes it clear that homework is an integral part of CT and not an optional extra depending upon the time available at the end of a session. Therefore, it is important that you make adequate provision for homework-setting and the initiation of the task in the structure of the session – perhaps 10 or 15 minutes, or even longer for novice CTers. If a clinically suitable homework task has emerged earlier in therapy and has been agreed upon, then obviously you will require less time at the end of the session to discuss it again. Always ensure that you give your clients a written copy of the homework task: this reminds them of what they have agreed to do and lessens the chances of their forgetting to do it. If the task is just agreed orally it may cause disagreements at the next session:

Therapist: We agreed that you were going to carry out the assignment on a daily basis. Remember?

Client: No, not the way I remember it. I agreed to do the assignment every other day.

Therapist: I'm sure you're mistaken about that.

Client: I'm sure I'm not.

If this kind of scenario occurs, do not waste valuable therapy time arguing about it. Instead, congratulate clients on what they actually carried out and elicit from them any learning gained. Then ensure that the next homework assignments are written down.

Collaborating with Paul on homework setting

In Chapter 3, one of Paul's adaptive responses to his NATs was, 'The less I do the more helpless I feel. That's the real problem. So I'll get over my helplessness by doing more'. It seemed a logical step to discuss homework tasks based on greater activity:

Paul: That would help a lot. I'm already doing more and more around the house.

Therapist: Would you like to do more outside of the house?

Paul: Yes I would. I used to be quite fit but when I became depressed I didn't bother about that any longer.

Therapist: Okay. Let's fill in this homework assignment sheet (Figure 4.1).

It's important to write down the assignment and for each of us to have a copy so we are both sure what has been agreed.

Paul: Sounds sensible.

Therapist: So looking at the sheet, 'What is the assignment?' What would you like to do outside the house?

Paul: I would like to go out for a walk each day, two walks per day if possible. Morning and afternoon.

Therapist: For how long would you go out on each occasion?

Paul: Er, 30 minutes minimum and 45 minutes maximum.

Therapist: Write that down please.

Paul: 'Twice-daily walks to the local park and back. Minimum 30 minutes and maximum 45 minutes.'

Therapist: The next question on the sheet is 'What is the purpose of the assignment?'

Paul: Well, if I do more things this will make me feel less helpless, get fitter and more interested in the world around me.

Therapist: If you feel less helpless, what will you feel more of then?

Paul: More hopeful.

Therapist: How will this assignment tackle your depression?

Paul: Being active instead of inactive is helping me to shake off this depression. That book you lent me, *Feeling Good*, went on about how important daily activity is.

Therapist: Good. So if you fill in the purpose of the assignment. . .

Paul: 'It will help me to feel less helpless and more hopeful. Also fitter and more interested in the world around me. These things will help me to shake off my depression.'

Therapist: The next heading looks at 'Obstacles to carrying out the assignment and ways to overcome them'.

Paul: Well, the only real obstacle might be not having the motivation to go out for the walks because I'll tell myself I'm not in the mood. I know I'll feel better after them but it's just getting going. That'll be the problem.

Therapist: Now, as you've been reading *Feeling Good*, do you remember what David Burns says about action and motivation?

Paul: It was something about action comes first and then motivation follows on once you are doing something, not the other way round.

Therapist: Would that help you get going when you don't feel like it?

Paul: I think it would. So I'll write down the obstacle as 'Not being motivated' and I'll tackle that by saying 'Get moving! Motivation will come later'.

Therapist: Any other obstacles?

Paul: No, that's it at the present time.

Therapist: The last heading is 'Contingency plan if assignment proves too difficult or overwhelming to accomplish'. What could you do if, for any reason, you were unable to carry out the above assignment?

Paul: I might be able to manage 10 or 15 minutes twice daily, or only once a day, or even every other day. I'd do whatever I can.

Therapist: Good. That's the point: whatever you can. And what could you note down that prevents you from carrying out the assignment or even any part of it?

Paul: Write down the thoughts and feelings that hold me back.

Therapist: And we can discuss those at the next session. So if you will fill in the last section please.

Paul: Okay. 'Do what I can. Write down thoughts and feelings that hold me back.'

Therapist: Now, whenever possible, it's important to start the assignment in the session, to give you a nudge so to speak. Now you usually come by bus to the session. How long would it take you to walk home from here?

Paul: About 30–40 minutes I guess.

Therapist: Would you like to start the assignment by walking home? This could count as your morning walk.

Paul: Okay. I didn't expect that but I'd certainly like to give it a go. If I start flagging, I can always jump on the bus.

Therapist: One last thing: can you phone me when you get home to see how you got on?

[This provides further encouragement for the client as well as checking on if he arrived home safely.]

Paul: No problem. See you next week then.

Therapist: Good luck.

Homework assignments are usually agreed at the end of a session and are reviewed at the beginning of the next one. With regard to a typical session agenda, homework usually provides the first and last items for discussion (session feedback is probably the very last item).

Reviewing homework assignments

At the beginning of every session, ask clients about their homework assignments. Neglecting to do this creates three problems:

> First, the patients usually begin to think that the homework is not important and, therefore, that treatment is something done to them rather than something they actively work on even in the absence of the therapist. Second, the therapists miss opportunities to correct mistakes such as the patients' inadequately responding rationally to their automatic thoughts. Third, the

---

HOMEWORK ASSIGNMENT SHEET

1. **What is the assignment? (State when, where and how often assignment is to be carried out.)**

   Twice daily walks to the local park and back. Minimum 30 minutes and maximum 45 minutes.

2. **What is the purpose of the assignment? (This should follow on from the session and be linked to the client's goals.)**

   It will help me to feel less helpless and more hopeful. Also fitter and more interested in the world around me. These things will help me shake off my depression.

3. **Obstacles to carrying out the assignment and ways to overcome them.**

   a.   Not being motivated – Get moving! Motivation will come later.
   b.
   c.

4. **Contingency plan if assignment proves too difficult or overwhelming to accomplish.**

   Do what I can. Write down thoughts and feelings that hold me back.

Figure 4.1: Paul's completed homework sheet.

therapists lose the chance to draw helpful lessons from the homework and to reinforce these lessons (Beck et al., 1993, p. 109).

Of course, if a crisis emerges (such as a client feeling suicidal) this has to be dealt with immediately and homework discussion is suspended; if there is time left in the session once the crisis has abated then return to a review of the homework. Precise information about homework needs to be elicited by you, such as what clients actually did or did not do, blocks to homework completion, any lessons that have been learned and conclusions drawn. Do not review homework in general terms, as in the following example, because this is valueless both to you and clients:

Therapist: Did you do the homework?

Client: Yeah, I did.

Therapist: Everything okay?

Client: Yeah, it was all right.

Therapist: Any hassles about doing it?

Client: I suppose it went all right, more or less.

Therapist: Good. Let's move on then.

Instead of skimming over discussion of the homework assignment, reviewing it in detail not only emphasizes its importance but also communicates to your clients genuine interest in their progress:

Therapist: How did you get on with your homework task, which was to decline your mother's invitation to spend Christmas with her as you have other plans this year?

Client: Well, it was only partly successful. I phoned her up and instead of saying I can't come this Christmas, I said I might not be able to make it.

Therapist: What thoughts prevented you from saying 'I can't come this Christmas'?

Client: Well, I thought 'If I don't see her this Christmas, she will be very hurt. I'll be responsible for that and feel bad about it'.

Therapist: Okay, those were your thoughts. Now what thoughts might your mother have about you not coming this Christmas that lead her to feel very hurt?

Client: Something like 'I can't enjoy Christmas without my daughter. She's let me down. What a way to treat her mother'. I know what you're getting at: people are responsible for how they think and the way they react to things, which is what CT is all about. I forgot that when I was talking to her.

Therapist: So how would you now respond to your automatic thoughts on this issue?

Client: 'My mother is not prepared to compromise over this issue, so if she feels hurt, that is due to her, not me. Of course, I don't want to see my mother upset, but this year I have got other plans which I'm keeping to.' That should help me to feel less bad about the situation.

Therapist: How can you check if that will be the case?

Client: Well, this time for homework I'm not going to waver, but to tell her I can't come this Christmas and explain the reasons why. If she doesn't want to hear my point of view, then so be it.

Therapist: We can review the outcome next week.

In the above extract, examination of the reasons for the client's partial completion of the homework assignment suggested ways of making its execution more successful at the next attempt. In the next example, the therapist seeks to capitalize on the client's successful homework completion:

Therapist: You seem very pleased about something.

Client: The homework went great. I got into the lift and went up two floors on my own, but I went further than we agreed and went down again. It wasn't as bad as I thought.

Therapist: That's great news. So what was going through your mind to urge you on?

Client: 'Just because I feel nervous, it doesn't mean there's going to be a catastrophe in the lift. So stay put and see what happens.' Nothing happened!

Therapist: Now, when we first discussed your lift phobia, the strategy was going to be slow and gradual. In the light of your great success, would you like to keep to that strategy or try something more ambitious?

Client: I feel I could go up to the top floor – the building has ten floors – and down again in one go. I feel very confident.

Therapist: That sounds fine. What would happen if you couldn't achieve that?

Client: I wouldn't be upset. I'm aiming for the top but anything short of that will be all right with me.

Therapist: Do you want to write that inspirational message down on a card and carry it with you in the lift?

Client: Yes, good idea.

Therapists' reactions to homework non-compliance

If clients do not carry out their homework assignments, your own thoughts and feelings might need to be monitored. For example, you may get angry because you believe clients 'are not pulling their weight' or you feel anxious that continuing non-compliance from clients will prove that you are an incompetent therapist. Obviously you will need to examine your own automatic thoughts and make adaptive responses to them (for example, 'My competence as a therapist is not dependent on whether clients carry out their assignments') before you can regain your clinical focus on tackling clients' impediments to homework completion.

'Doing the homework is critical for the therapeutic process to be effective. It is particularly important that clients understand this fact' (Walen, DiGiuseppe and Dryden, 1992, p. 272). By tackling their problems *in vivo*, clients learn the necessary skills for present and future problem-solving; that is, they learn to become their own therapists.

Up to this point in the book, therapy has focused on identifying and responding to NATs. In the next chapter, we trace the source of these NATs to underlying assumptions and core beliefs.

Chapter Five
Identifying and Examining Underlying Assumptions and Core Beliefs

In this chapter, techniques for identifying underlying beliefs are described. These include looking for common themes in clients' negative thinking, use of the downward arrow technique, and asking clients what their beliefs are. Methods for modifying underlying assumptions and rules include weighing their advantages and disadvantages, conducting behavioural experiments and questioning the validity of the personal contract. Schema-changing procedures focus on three key methods:

- continuum use
- positive data logs
- historical tests of core beliefs

Underlying beliefs

These were discussed in Chapter 1, but to refresh your memory: there are two categories of underlying beliefs. First, 'underlying assumptions' (conditional beliefs) and rules ('should' and 'must' statements) provide guidelines for how we operate in the world and what we expect to happen to us (for example, 'If I do what others want, then they'll like me', 'I should always try to please others'). As long as the conditions of these assumptions are met and rules are adhered to, individuals can remain relatively happy and stable. Second, 'core beliefs', the deepest level of cognition, are fundamental appraisals of ourselves ('I'm no good'), others ('No one can be trusted') and the world ('Everything is against me').

Negative and dysfunctional core beliefs are rigid and overgeneralized and are usually activated in times of emotional distress (they usually remain latent otherwise). Once activated, they determine how we view a situation and 'shut out' any information that may contradict it. How do these two belief levels interact? If the terms of the assumptions are not met (for example, despite always trying to please others, the person is rejected by some of his friends) this activates and confirms his core belief of worthlessness. Activated beliefs are often accompanied by painful affect, such as depression and hurt. Underlying beliefs are usually formed earlier in life, often remain unspoken (which is why they are referred to as 'silent assumptions') and therapy may be the first time they are made explicit.

Exploring underlying beliefs occurs when clients have gained some skill and confidence in applying the cognitive model to their problems by answering their NATs and have some completed homework assignments under their belt (though working on NATs 'chips away' at underlying beliefs). To tackle underlying beliefs before this stage has been reached may result in clients feeling overwhelmed, threatened, distressed or resistant; 'going too deep, too early' can result in premature termination of therapy (it is interesting to compare this gradualist approach to uncovering and examining beliefs with the approach of Rational Emotive Behaviour Therapy (Ellis, 1994) which zeroes in on core beliefs from the first session onwards). Techniques for identifying underlying assumptions, rules and core beliefs are now described. We shall take each belief level in turn.

Identifying underlying assumptions and rules

Revealing 'if ... then' statements

Clients often express their assumptions in 'if ... then' terms (for example, 'If I keep quiet in groups then I won't be the centre of attention and be picked on'). In the following dialogue, the therapist is on the lookout for dysfunctional assumptions and bringing them to the client's attention. Identifying such assumptions is the first step in beginning to change them:

Client: I've been pushing myself really hard to prepare for the talk to the consultants next week. I feel I'm on top of my subject and should be relaxed about the talk but I can't seem to wind down. If the preparation and planning are spot on, then the talk should be successful. So why am I still so anxious?

Therapist: Do you think there is a negative assumption at work here that is fuelling your anxiety? The other side of the assumption coin, so to speak.

Client: Hmm. Maybe the preparation and planning aren't spot on.

Therapist: If the preparation and planning are not spot on then . . .?

[Beck (1995) suggests that one way to elicit a full assumption is for the therapist to provide the first half of it.]

Client: ... then the talk will be a complete and utter disaster.

Therapist: So which assumption are you focused on?

Client: Obviously the negative one. I usually prepare to do my best yet assume the worst. Anything important I have do, I often get paralysed with anxiety about.

Therapist: So does this negative assumption operate in other areas of your life as well?

Client: Absolutely. I can sum it up more accurately: 'If it's not done perfectly, then it's crap!'

Pinpointing 'shoulds' and 'musts'

Personal rules are often expressed in 'should' and 'must' statements ('I should never show my feelings', 'I must have the respect of others'). As the examples show, these rules can be seen as maladaptive because they do not allow for flexibility if the rules are violated or standards are not maintained. Clients can learn to spot the 'shoulds' and 'musts' in their thinking once these are brought to their attention or are emphasized by the therapist:

Client: I feel guilty for upsetting my son. I promised to take him swimming then something important came up and I had to cancel it at the last minute. He was upset. If I promise something, I should always keep to it.

Therapist: It's regrettable that you couldn't take your son swimming and he got upset about it, but are you aware of what you just said about promises?

Client: Of course, I should always keep them.

Therapist: (emphasizes) 'Should always keep them.' Do you think you are being excessively hard on yourself?

Client: No. I should be hard on myself if I break a promise. I don't like feeling guilty though.

Therapist: Well, rigid 'shoulds' expressed as rules usually do lead to some kind of upset when these rules are not followed; hence the hard time you give yourself.

Client: That's true. Thinking about it now, I do use that word a lot.

Therapist: Shall we see how many 'shoulds' we can spot before the end of the session and maybe you can also keep a diary for the next seven days noting how many 'should' statements you make?

Client: Okay to both ideas. (laughs) That should be interesting.

Discerning themes in clients' automatic thoughts

You can review with your clients their dysfunctional thought records (DTRs) in order to discern recurring themes in their patterns of thinking. For example, a sample of a client's automatic thoughts are: 'I need to ensure that people see me in the right way', 'I've got to make sure that everything is just right' and 'Things have to run smoothly'. You can ask clients if they are aware of a theme(s) running through their thoughts, or suggest one yourself:

Therapist: In looking at your thoughts on these forms, can you make out a particular theme that connects these thoughts?

Client: I'm not sure what you mean?

Therapist: In doing this exercise with some other clients, they have identified themes of failure or rejection in their thoughts.

Client: Oh, I see. Hmm. I'm not sure.

Therapist: There seems to be a theme of the need for control in your life.

Client: Absolutely.

Therapist: What will happen if you don't have this control?

Client: I believe that unless I do have control over things in my life, everything is going to fall apart.

[The client's assumption has been located.]

Marked mood variations

Fennell (1989, p. 204) suggests that 'high mood often indicates that the terms of an assumption have been met, just as low mood signals its violation'. For example, these high and low moods can be observed with homework tasks and reflected back to the client to tease out the assumption:

Therapist: You're in high spirits today.

Client: Yeah, I cracked it. The homework was a piece of cake.

Therapist: What does it mean to you to have 'cracked it'?

Client: When I put my mind to something, then I carry it through.

A few weeks later, the same client had trouble carrying out an assignment and appeared dejected:

Therapist: You seem very low.

Client: The homework was a mess.

Therapist: What does that mean to you when the homework is 'a mess'?

Client: When I can't get my mind on something, nothing works for me.

Use of imagery to uncover assumptions

Asking clients the meanings attached to their images can provide clues to underlying beliefs (remember that some clients may experience negative appraisals of events more powerfully in images rather than thoughts). For example, a client who was very anxious about a forthcoming presentation had a very vivid image of herself, when she made a mistake, getting smaller and smaller in front of her audience. When asked what this image meant to her, she replied:

Client: I'm reduced to a state of nothingness.

Therapist: How does making a mistake lead to a state of nothingness?

Client: Because if I make a mistake in front of others, then my credibility as an authority on the subject completely collapses.

Ask the client

As we have said, underlying beliefs are frequently unarticulated and therefore have to be inferred from client clues (such as recurring themes in their communications). However, it should not be overlooked that the most obvious and straightforward way to elicit an assumption or rule is to ask the client:

Therapist: We've looked at a number of situations where you put others first and yourself second. Is there a particular belief that guides your behaviour in these situations?

Client: My parents taught me that I should always put others first and not to do so is a sign of selfishness.

Therapist: Have you always followed that rule?

Client: All my life.

Belief questionnaires

These act as another straightforward way of eliciting silent assumptions through the use of belief questionnaires such as the *Dysfunctional Attitude Scale* (DAS) (Weissman and Beck, 1978). The DAS is a 100-item self-report scale which focuses on such areas as approval, love, achievement, perfectionism and entitlement. The DAS may be used in addition to the other techniques in this section to identify dysfunctional underlying beliefs.

The downward arrow technique (Burns, 1980)

This involves asking clients to identify an important automatic thought (usually a hot one) and then asking them 'What does that mean to you?' in order to uncover another thought, and the same question (or a variation of it, such as 'If that's true, then what?') is asked again. Through this process, layers of thoughts are peeled back until an underlying or core belief is revealed. As Beck et al. (1993, p. 140) observe:

> Many patients are unable to articulate these underlying beliefs until they have been asked to consider the personal *meaning* that their more manifest thoughts have for them. Therefore, when patients exhibit strong negative emotions that seem to be far more intense than their automatic thoughts alone would cause . . .

You can use the downward arrow to trace the cognitive source of this strong affect. Unlike responding to automatic thoughts, each thought is accepted as temporarily true until a belief is revealed. In the following example, a client is very anxious about going out with a new boyfriend as she believes 'I know it won't work out' (automatic thought):

Therapist: What does that mean to you if it doesn't work out?

Client: That he doesn't like me.

Therapist: And if that is true, then what?

Client: Here we go again.

Therapist: What does that mean to you 'here we go again'?

Client: That I'm always going to be on my own.

Therapist: And what does that mean to you?

Client: (tearful) That no matter how hard I try, I'm always going to be on my own because no one really likes or wants me [underlying assumption].

Beck (1995, p. 145) points out that 'asking what a thought means to the patient [or to his view of others or the world] often elicits an intermediate belief [assumption or rule]; asking what it means about the patient [others or the world] usually uncovers the core belief' (we shall use the downward arrow later in this chapter to reveal a core belief). When you have identified clients' feelings (anxiety in the above example), do not ask further questions about them as this will lead to a focus on feelings instead of an investigation into the meaning of clients' thoughts connected to their feelings:

Therapist: What does it mean to you when you feel hurt?

Client: I hate feeling like that.

Therapist: And what does that mean to you?

Client: Well, as I said, I hate feeling hurt.

Therapist: And if that's true, what then?

Client: I just mope around the house feeling sorry for myself. I don't know what else to say. I feel hurt.

Instead of a downward arrow, both therapist and client are going round in a circle. This results in confusion and a loss of therapeutic focus, not uncovering beliefs. The therapist in the example should have elicited thoughts connected to the client's hurt (for example, 'What thoughts are going through your mind when you feel hurt?' Reply: 'My friends let me down.'). The therapist should then have pursued the personal meanings of being 'let down' in order to reveal the client's underlying assumption: 'If your friends let you down, then you can never trust anyone again'.

Identifying Paul's underlying assumptions

As Paul gained skill in identifying, examining and responding to his NATs, his mood improved (as reflected in his lower scores on the Beck Depression Inventory and Hopelessness Scale). As he could see and agreed with the applicability of the cognitive model to addressing his problems, therapy moved on to focusing on deeper cognitive levels:

Therapist: These automatic thoughts we've been looking at over the past weeks, and you've been answering, spring from deeper beliefs that you have but may be not always aware of.

Paul: That makes sense.

Therapist: Let me draw this relationship on the whiteboard.

Automatic thoughts

↑

Underlying assumptions

↑

Core beliefs

The next step is to look at the level of underlying assumptions which, in contrast to the situation-specific automatic thoughts, usually connect many situations.

Paul: Didn't we talk about those several sessions ago?

Therapist: During the assessment, we noted down a few assumptions [see Chapter 2]. To see if they are still accurate, or maybe find more important ones, we could try a technique called the downward arrow. If you can suggest an important negative automatic thought that pops into your head when you're feeling down, I'll demonstrate this technique.

Paul: (laughs) That's easy: 'No one wants to be around a failure'.

Therapist: What does that mean to you that 'no one wants to be around a failure'?

Paul: I've let everybody down by not measuring up to their standards.

Therapist: And if that's true, what then?

Paul: Then I've let everyone down because of my failure and they will reject me (hanging his head down).

Therapist: So is the assumption 'If I don't measure up to their standards, then I've let everyone down because of my failure and they will reject me'.

Paul: That's right.

Therapist: (reading the assessment form) That's pretty much what you said on the assessment form, apart from bringing shame on yourself and your family.

Paul: Well that's true isn't it? I suppose it's true.

Therapist: Let's discuss it and see if we can put that to the test in some way and come up with a more reasonable response to that assumption in the same way you did with your automatic thoughts.

Paul: Okay. Let's hope it works again.

Examining underlying assumptions and rules

Behavioural experiments

Padesky (1994) suggests that underlying assumptions are usually best tested through the use of behavioural experiments. For example, a client who believes 'If I make a mistake in front of others then they will laugh at me for being an idiot' agrees to make some deliberate mistakes to verify if others do actually laugh at him; another client who believes 'If I put myself first sometimes, other people will see me as selfish and despise me' declares to others what he wants to do and checks with them to determine if he is now despised or seen as selfish.

Behavioural experiments are a powerful way of modifying dysfunctional assumptions and helping clients to produce more adaptive alternatives (for example, 'If I make a mistake in front of others, perhaps one or two will laugh at me for being an idiot but most probably won't'). Fennell (1989, p. 207) suggests that 'alternatives to dysfunctional assumptions can be written on flash-cards for patients to read repeatedly until acting in accordance with them becomes second nature'.

Validity of the personal contract (Blackburn and Davidson, 1995)

This refers to clients reviewing the terms of the personal contracts (assumptions, rules) they have constructed in their heads. For example, a client considered whether her own contract 'If I help others, then they must help me' realistically reflected her relationships with others; and if she rewrote the contract, she might not experience the bitter disappointment she usually endured when others let her down (i.e. she would stop demanding that the terms of the contract *must* be fulfilled). Eventually, she decided that a more realistic and helpful assumption would be 'If I help others, which I like to do, then I should not automatically expect them to help me, but it would be nice if they did sometimes'. Burns (1980) calls this technique 'rewriting the rules'.

Listing the advantages and disadvantages

Clients can be encouraged to list and examine the advantages and disadvantages of holding a particular assumption or rule. In the following example, the client's assumption is written on the whiteboard and then the board is divided into two columns (this list is not meant to be exhaustive):

Assumption: 'If I don't get close to others, then I won't get hurt'

Advantages	Disadvantages
1. 'Keeps me safe'	1. 'I miss closeness and intimacy'
2. 'Avoid rejection'	2. 'But I also avoid having a relationship'
3. 'I have emotional control'	3. 'Do I? Then why do I get depressed about being on my own?'
	4. 'Living the rest of my life on my own'
	5. 'If I don't learn to cope with my hurt feelings, I'll never grow up'

As usually happens with this technique, disadvantages eventually outweigh advantages (though you may need to tease out the disadvantages as clients often pinpoint the advantages more readily than the drawbacks). Also, you can ask clients to re-evaluate whether the advantages are really beneficial, as they often turn out to be illusory. For example:

Therapist: It seems very powerful having emotional control.

Client: Yeah, it does seem so I suppose.

Therapist: You don't sound convinced.

Client: Emotional control is the same thing as feeling dead inside. What's the point of having control if you are not enjoying life?

With disadvantages outweighing advantages, and some of the advantages revealed as self-defeating, clients are likely to initiate personal change and thereby develop a more functional assumption, such as 'Getting close to others may involve getting hurt but this is a price worth paying for the pleasure of a relationship. If I do get hurt, I can learn to cope with it differently than in the past'. This technique is also known as a 'cost–benefit analysis'.

Historical development of assumptions and rules

Clients can profit from learning about the development of their dysfunctional assumptions and rules in order to understand how they arrived at their present position in life (Scott, Stradling and Dryden, 1995). This development usually starts early in life (but not inevitably so) as children form beliefs in the light of their experiences and relationships with others.

For example, a child who has angry and unpredictable parents believes 'If I always do as I'm told, then my parents won't shout at me and make me cry'. This belief may have appeared adaptive as a child in order to avoid parental anger, but in adulthood this belief has become maladaptive as the client is submissive in her relationships ('I don't like being like that but I'm still wary of people being angry with me').

By comparing and contrasting the operation of the assumption in childhood and adulthood, the client can reassess if the same unpleasant consequences hold today if 'I don't always do as I'm told'. Such discussion encourages clients to develop more realistic and moderate assumptions (such as 'I can learn to be assertive in my relationships when it's necessary and see if people really will be angry with me for doing so. If they are, then this is something I need to deal with. I don't want to see myself any longer as a child afraid of grown-ups').

Use of imagery

Clients may experience distressing images but 'stop the film' just before or at the moment the catastrophe occurs, thereby not allowing themselves to see 'what happened next' and if adaptive imagery can be visualized. For example, a client believes that 'If I faint in public, people will laugh at me because they'll think I'm drunk or something like that' and freezes the imagery at the point of fainting. The therapist guides the client beyond this point and helps her to arrive at a different interpretation of the situation:

Therapist: Close your eyes and imagine you've collapsed in the high street. What's going on right now?

Client: I'm lying on the ground unconscious. I've passed out. There are people around me, pointing and laughing at me.

Therapist: How will you know if they are laughing at you if you are unconscious?

Client: I don't know. I never thought of that.

Therapist: How long will you be unconscious for?

Client: Only a minute or two.

Therapist: What do you see when you open your eyes? Anyone laughing?

Client: No, they're not doing that. People are asking me if I'm all right and do I need a doctor.

Therapist: Can you hear if anyone is whispering that you are a drunk or something like that?

[The client's prediction that she will be seen as a 'drunk or something like that' if she faints in front of others is being tested.]

Client: No, I can't hear that.

Therapist: What happens next?

Client: People are helping me to my feet and picking up my shopping and putting it back into the shopping bag for me.

Therapist: And once you are on your feet, what happens then?

Client: People are still asking me if I'm all right, then they go about their business. I walk home, a bit unsteady on my feet.

Therapist: How are you feeling now?

Client: Not so worried about fainting in public.

Therapist: What's changed for you then?

Client: Well, if I faint people are more likely to help me than laugh at me or call me names. It does seem a much more realistic picture of the way things will turn out.

Therapist: You'll need to practise this imagery exercise in order to strengthen in your mind this more realistic outcome.

Wells (1997, p. 77) suggests:

> in some cases merely staying with an image or simply suggesting running the image forward or backward in time is all that is required for a spontaneous modification to take place. When a more spontaneous change seems unlikely the therapist should take a more active role in manipulating the contents of the image.

Developing an alternative assumption that retains the advantages of the maladaptive assumption and avoids its disadvantages (Fennell, 1989)

Maladaptive assumptions are often constructed in rigid and excessive terms. For example, a client believes 'If I don't maintain my high standards, then I'm incompetent'; when he falls below his high standards, this triggers a bout of depression. The client acknowledges the need to change the assumption but fears that his standards will plummet as a consequence. After discussion with the therapist, the client devises an alternative assumption that keeps the 'good' parts of the old one and removes the 'bad' parts. Thus: 'I shall continue to do my best to maintain my high standards but if I fall below them at times, I will not condemn myself as incompetent. Instead, I will focus on what went wrong and how to put it right if I can.' This new assumption helped the client to reduce considerably his bouts of depression when he fell below his high standards.

Modification of the 'shoulds' (Beck et al., 1979)

Rules of living are often expressed in absolute 'shoulds' ('I should always be the first in the office and the last out, otherwise my colleagues will see me as a slacker'). One way to challenge the 'should' is by disobeying it in order to evaluate the consequences and thereby provide opportunities to modify it. In the above example, on some days the client goes to work later and leaves earlier than his colleagues. To the client's surprise, his colleagues congratulate him on 'starting to look after yourself instead of overdoing it' and state they have never regarded him as a slacker, 'far from it'. By disobeying the rule, the client is able to ease the internal pressure he has always put himself under, and discovers that there is more to life than consistently long hours at the office.

Contrasting the short- and long-term helpfulness of personal rules and assumptions

Clients frequently focus on the immediate or short-term beneficial effects to be derived from subscribing to a particular rule or assumption at the expense of looking at its longer-term harmful or self-defeating effects. Beck et al. (1979, p. 270) state that it is particularly important to look at these longer-term effects:

> when the dysfunctional assumption currently appears to be working in the person's favor. That is, many who believe that they need the approval of everyone are often extremely happy when they think they have this approval.

Like the stock exchange, their personal value rises when people invest in them (i.e. they receive others' approval) and it falls or nosedives when people disinvest in them (i.e. others withdraw their approval). Such individuals need to look ahead to see the emotional distress they may experience when people disinvest in them and start constructing *now* more helpful assumptions that avoid making their self-worth conditional (for example, 'It's currently very nice to have people's approval, but it's not essential. If some people turn against me later, I can still accept myself, whatever happens').

Examining Paul's underlying assumptions

In the previous dialogue with Paul, a key dysfunctional assumption of his was identified: 'If I don't measure up to their standards, then I've let everyone down because of my failure and they will reject me'. The following discussion with him examines the validity of this assumption:

Therapist: When you say that everyone will reject you because of your failure, does that include your wife?

Paul: Yes, but I also know that's silly because she hasn't rejected me.

Therapist: Why do you think that is?

Paul: Because she doesn't see me as a failure.

Therapist: Have you asked her?

Paul: Not directly, but I know you're going to ask me to. I will do it and it won't be a problem for me.

Therapist: So you can strike one person off your list of everyone who will reject you. Now who will it be a problem asking?

Paul: (voice drops) My parents.

Therapist: You think they really will reject you as failure because you don't measure up to their standards?

Paul: I'm sure of it.

Therapist: You haven't told them about your company going bust and your becoming depressed over it.

Paul: Not yet. I feel I should but I worry about their reaction.

Therapist: You seem so convinced it will turn out badly for you.

Paul: I am.

Therapist: If we can go back in time, did they reject you when you got a 2:1 instead of the expected first-class degree?

Paul: Well, I thought they did. I kept in my bedroom a lot or came home late so they would be in bed when I got in.

Therapist: Did you withdraw from them or did they withdraw from you?

Paul: Well, I ... (seeming uncertain) I suppose I withdrew from them because I thought they would reject me.

Therapist: So you got in first, so to speak.

Paul: Seems so.

Therapist: Did they say anything to you during that period?

Paul: They asked me if I was all right, did I need anything, things like that. My parents are not what you would call very emotional, they're rather reserved in their manner.

Therapist: But in their own way, do you think they cared about you during that period, or had they rejected you?

Paul: You see, I'm not sure now with these questions you're asking me. They probably cared for me. However, I'm sure they were very disappointed.

Therapist: For you or in you?

Paul: Up to now, I would have thought 'in me', but again I'm not so sure. Probably they were disappointed for me in not getting a first after all the hard work I put in.

Therapist: In the light of our discussion, do you think you might be mistaken about how your parents will react if you tell them about your present problems?

Paul: I could well be, and there is only one way to find out – tell them.

Therapist: Do you feel ready to do that?

Paul: I think so. It will help me to clear up a number of issues both past and present.

Therapist: So is that your next homework task: to tell your parents?

Paul: It is. I will do so this weekend.

Identifying core beliefs

Some of the same techniques are used for identifying core beliefs as for underlying assumptions (such as discerning themes in clients' automatic thoughts, asking the client). In this section the downward arrow technique is demonstrated again, and we look at the additional techniques of 'sentence-completion' and 'conjunctive phrasing'.

The downward arrow

This technique begins with the identification of an important automatic thought and the meaning of this and subsequent thoughts is elicited until a core belief is uncovered. In the following example, a client is anxious about her husband's increasing lateness from work, as this might indicate he is having an affair:

Therapist: What would that mean to you?

Client: That he doesn't love me any more.

Therapist: And if he doesn't, what then?

Client: He'll leave me.

Therapist: And if he does. . .?

Client: I'll be all alone, abandoned.

Therapist: And what does that mean about you?

[Asking clients 'What does that mean about you?' instead of 'to you?' usually reveals a core belief.]

Client: That I'm undesirable, repulsive [core belief].

Sentence-completion

You can write on your whiteboard or a piece of paper the following incomplete sentences and ask your clients to 'fill in the blanks' in order to identify their core beliefs about themselves, others and the world:

- I am ... (weak)
- People are ... (threatening)
- The world is ... (dangerous)

Another example of sentence-completion would be for the client to arrive at a core belief aided by the therapist's prompting:

Client: I'm scared stiff about giving that workshop and it all going wrong.

Therapist: You're scared stiff of it all going wrong because. . .?

Client: That will prove I'm a crap trainer [core belief].

Conjunctive phrasing

This refers to the use of phrases such as 'and therefore. . .' or 'and if that is true. . .' or 'and then. . .' to 'nudge along' clients' train of thought to its conclusion. The therapist removes the full stop at the end of a client's sentence and replaces it with a conjunction:

Client: I might not be able to do the job properly.

Therapist: And then. . .?

Client: It would be a big mess.

Therapist: And if it was. . .?

Client: I'd be totally incompetent [core belief].

DiGiuseppe (1991a, p. 168) observes that an 'advantage of this method is that it keeps clients focused on their thoughts. The less a therapist says, the less clients have to respond to the therapist's words or attend to whether the therapist has understood them. The conjunctive phrase focuses clients on the meaning of their statements'. We have used the term 'verbal economy' to convey the same point as DiGiuseppe's (Neenan and Dryden, 2000). Verbal economy should also be the guiding principle while using the downward arrow method.

Identifying Paul's core beliefs

From the first session onwards, Paul was quite clear that his core belief about himself was 'I'm a failure'. However, when focusing on core beliefs took centre stage in therapy, Paul now seemed uncertain:

Therapist: It was one of the first things you said to me – that you were a failure.

Paul: I know, but we've done a lot of work since then and it doesn't feel quite right any more. It's something else. It's more than just being a failure.

Therapist: Okay. Let's see if we can find out. What does it mean to you to be a failure?

Paul: I've let others down.

Therapist: And if you have. . .?

Paul: Then I don't deserve their love and respect.

Therapist: Because. . .?

Paul: (emphatic) I'm not good enough. That's it. That feels exactly right. That's what's been driving me and troubling me all these years: at bottom, I've never believed I am good enough.

Therapist: Do you think that others will reject you for not being good enough?

Paul: Yes, I believe that too: I'm not good enough and others will will see it and reject me because of it.

Therapist: So we have two core beliefs about yourself and others to work on and change.

In the light of this new information, Paul's case conceptualization (see Chapter 2) was altered to incorporate it (no core beliefs about the world were uncovered). These were the only significant alterations to the initial case conceptualization.

Teaching clients about the formation and maintenance of core beliefs

Core beliefs (or schemas) are usually formed in the light of early learning experiences. They can be both positive ('I'm competent') and negative ('I'm incompetent'); most people have both. They process incoming information and thereby determine how we perceive events; in a sense, we can see only what core beliefs allow us to. Negative core beliefs are often activated and thereby pass into our awareness at times of emotional distress or during traumatic events (for example, a client whose wife leaves him believes 'I'm worthless without her'). With such a schema activated, any information or experience that contradicts the schema is likely to be dismissed, distorted or overlooked (Padesky and Greenberger, 1995). With regard to the above example, the client refuses to accept any suggestions from others that he is still valued by them, as such discrepant information would not 'fit into' his activated schema of worthlessness.

Chapter 1 discussed the three main ways core beliefs are perpetuated. We now return to this discussion and expand upon it. Young (1994; Young and Lindemann, 1992) has focused upon the 'schema processes, or coping styles, [that] serve both to maintain the validity of the schema and to avoid experiencing the painful affect associated with schema activation. *Schema Maintenance, Schema Avoidance*, and *Schema Compensation* are the three broad forms of schema processes that are initially activated by, and ultimately reinforce, the schemata' [italics in original] (Young and Behary, 1998, p. 349). Clients may exhibit all three schema processes, but with some more prominent than others.

Schema maintenance

This refers to ways of thinking and behaving that perpetuate core beliefs. Young and Behary (1998, p. 349) suggest 'this can also be viewed as the patient's surrendering to the schema'. For example, a person who sees himself as inferior to others always puts himself, imaginally and literally, at the back of any queue ('I don't deserve any better').

Schema avoidance

This refers to the cognitive, behavioural and emotional strategies that individuals use to avoid activating core beliefs and the painful feelings associated with them. (For example, a woman drinks heavily to 'drown out' memories of the break-up of her relationship, and seeing herself as unwanted. However, through the act of avoidance she reminds herself she is unwanted.)

Schema compensation

This refers to behaviours in which clients engage that seem to contradict their core beliefs or overcompensate for them. (For example, an individual who sees himself as unlikeable does his best to build up a wide circle of friends and have a busy social life.)

> Schema compensation processes may be viewed as partially successful attempts by patients to challenge their schemas. Since it usually involves a failure to recognize the underlying vulnerability, it leaves the patient unprepared for the pain evoked when compensation fails and the schema is triggered (Young and Lindemann, 1992, p. 13).

In the above example, when his friends start to drift away and his social life shrinks correspondingly, this reinforces his self-image as unlikeable ('What the hell do I have to do to be liked?').

Educating Paul about his core beliefs

This educative approach reinforces collaboration and acts as a prelude to schema change.

Therapist: In peeling back the layers of your thinking we have reached the final destination of core beliefs – what David Burns calls 'the cause of it all'.

Paul: I haven't got to that chapter yet. I presume 'I'm not good enough' is my core belief and that's what does the damage.

Therapist: That's right. This belief helps to explain why you've been vulnerable to emotional problems in the past, why you are currently depressed and will remain vulnerable in the future to possible further periods of depression unless this belief is modified.

Paul: I've had that belief a long time.

Therapist: Core beliefs, we're only looking at negative ones here, are usually formed in childhood. They remain quiet, so to speak, when things are running relatively smoothly in our lives, but are activated or aroused when we run into emotional trouble; then they dominate how we see things by focusing on only what appears to support the belief and excluding any information that contradicts it.

Paul: That makes sense. I can think of lots of examples of that happening and, of course, my company going bust is just the recent example. I just saw everything as me not being good enough, I'll never be good enough [schema maintenance].

Therapist: That helps to explain how we keep these core beliefs going over the years. Have you ever tried to prove that you were actually good enough?

Paul: Sure. I used to knock myself out at times with all the work I took on to prove to myself that I was good enough and I would get people's respect and approval. Hard work equals respect equals being good enough. I've been trying hard to prove what I'm not for a long time [schema compensation].

Therapist: What usually happened?

Paul: Something would go wrong and I'd be back to square one, down in the dumps for a while.

Therapist: The strategy backfired, in other words.

Paul: That's what usually happened. I never checked to see if I had actually lost other people's respect and approval: I just assumed it.

Therapist: And did you try to avoid situations or doing things that might trigger the core belief and the bad feelings associated with it?

Paul: Well, when things backfired I certainly was more cautious about doing things where I might not measure up in some way. I tried to get out of things if I could. I didn't want to be exposed in that way [schema avoidance]. But the biggest thing driving me all these years is to prove that I'm good enough [compensation appears to be Paul's major schema process].

Therapist: My questions have been designed to show you the three major ways of perpetuating core beliefs. First, by looking for information that supports them; second, by avoiding triggering them; and third, trying to fight against them in order to prove the opposite, but something usually goes wrong and. . .

Paul: Back to square one.

Therapist: Exactly. Would you like to note down on a white card those three main ways of perpetuating core beliefs?

Paul: Okay, and I can go over them for homework. It's becoming clear to me now how this perpetuation process goes on, but what isn't clear is how I change it. How do I?

Developing alternative core beliefs

As soon as clients' key core beliefs have been identified and initial schema education has begun, it is important to identify and start developing alternative and more adaptive core beliefs in order for them, rather than the dysfunctional core beliefs, to be the centre of clinical attention (Padesky, 1994). As DiGiuseppe (1991b, p. 181) observes, examining dysfunctional beliefs is not sufficient to modify them:

> People frequently hold on to beliefs that they know are logically flawed and do not lead to accurate predictions of reality, but no alternative ideas are available to replace the flawed idea. The history of science is filled with such examples. People do not give up ideas, regardless of the evidence against the idea, unless they have an alternative idea to replace it.

Therefore develop alternative schemas as soon as possible once schema work begins:

Therapist: How would you like to see yourself instead of as not good enough?

Paul: I'd like to see myself as good enough in my own eyes, if that's possible.

Therapist: So what would good enough in your own eyes look like?

Paul: Well, I could accept both successes and setbacks, have strengths and weaknesses, deal with the usual ups and downs of life without putting myself on the line all the time, not take things personally. You know, just try to be on an even keel.

Therapist: How would you like to see others? You usually see them as rejecting you for not measuring up to their standards.

Paul: That's a lop-sided view and I know it's not true. (musing) So how would I like to see them? People can be rejecting but also very supportive and kind. I would like to have a balanced view of how I see others. I know people are not usually rejecting in my life. In fact, I'm hard put to think when I have actually been rejected, as crazy as it sounds.

Therapist: Okay. So we will start work on these two images of how you would like to see yourself and others. The general strategy will be weakening the old negative beliefs while simultaneously strengthening the new beliefs.

Examining and modifying core beliefs

Padesky (1994) suggests three key methods for schema change: use of a continuum, positive data logs and historical tests of a schemas.

Use of a continuum

Clients' core beliefs are often constructed in all-or-nothing terms (such as 'If I'm not a success, then I'm a failure'). The use of a continuum (i.e. a scale from 0% to 100%) introduces shades of grey into clients' thinking, thereby helping them to develop more balanced and realistic appraisals of themselves, others and the world (to arrive eventually at the mid-point on the continuum). Padesky and Greenberger (1995, p. 144) state that:

> a scale or continuum is most therapeutic when it is constructed and its data evaluated for the new schema rather than the old. A small shift that strengthens the new schema is usually more hopeful for the client than a small shift that weakens the old schema.

For example, if schema change is evaluated along a continuum focusing on the old belief ('I'm worthless'), the client might declare that 'I'm only 80% worthless now', whereas if it is evaluated along a continuum of his alternative belief ('I'm worthwhile'), optimism can be encouraged by seeing himself as 20% worthwhile (and likely to increase over time). The 0%, 50% and 100% points on the continuum were defined by Paul as:

	I'm good enough	
0%	50%	100%
Barely adequate	Achievements and setbacks	Supreme confidence and success

When asked, in percentage terms, how good enough he was at the present time he replied 'ten per cent'. A cross was placed at 10% on the continuum. The rest of the session was spent discussing recent experiences (progress in therapy, business failure, telling his parents about his depression) as part of a rounded view of what 'good enough' means. At the end of the session, Paul decided 25% was a more reasonable figure for being good enough and another cross was added to the continuum. The continuum can be used regularly as a reference point to monitor clients' progress towards 'the middle ground' based on information collected from various sources (such as positive data logs).

Positive data logs

Keeping logs or diaries encourages clients to collect information over the weeks and months to support their new adaptive beliefs; this method reduces their tendency to discount positive information and focus only on information that endorses the old belief (information processing errors). Padesky (1993b) likens maladaptive core beliefs about oneself to self-prejudice: negative views of the self that are held firmly in the face of contradictory information. Such self-prejudice helps to maintain maladaptive schemas, as discussed with Paul:

Therapist: Negative core beliefs about oneself have been called a self-prejudice.

Paul: What do you mean?

Therapist: How would you see a person who has a prejudice?

Paul: Well, I suppose someone with a fixed point of view, not really interested in changing it or seeing anyone else's viewpoint.

Therapist: And holds on to it in the face of information that could discredit it.

Paul: We're talking about me, aren't we? I've believed I'm not good enough over the years and anything that may have challenged it I pushed aside or refused to believe it.

Therapist: And that's how a fixed belief or prejudice is maintained. Now, with these positive data logs it is important to look for information that supports your new belief 'I'm good enough'.

Paul: You mean you want me to train myself to see differently, so to speak. Remove my blinkers.

Therapist: How else will you overcome your self-prejudice? Will it wither away on its own?

Paul: It hasn't so far, has it? Okay, it will be an effort as I'm not used to it.

Therapist: That's true as you've only just pinpointed a new belief you would like to believe in, but try not to overlook any piece of positive information, no matter how small, that might support this belief.

Paul: Such as what? Can you give me an example?

Therapist: Has anything happened today or in the preceding week, for example, that might fit this new self-image of being good enough?

Paul: Hmm. Well, when I spoke to my parents the other week about my problems, which was the homework task – I feared they were going to disown me when I told them – but they were understanding, they wanted to help me. They told me I'm their son and they would never reject me. On the way home in the car, I was angry with myself: 'If they can accept me, then it's about time I did the same, so grow up!' I thought at that moment that it was possible to believe in myself.

Therapist: So can we put that down as the first piece of evidence to support your new belief?

Paul: We can.

When clients have little or no conviction in their new adaptive beliefs, it can be very difficult for them to extract any positive information from their daily experiences; therefore, you will need to be alert in every session to help them identify schema-supporting information.

Historical test of new schema

Maladaptive schemas are usually formed in childhood and therefore clients may have collected a great deal of evidence over the years to support them. Undertaking a retrospective survey of clients' lives can help them to uncover evidence that supports their new beliefs. Padesky (1994) suggests dividing clients' lives into time periods (for example 0–2, 3–5, 6–12 years) and recommends starting the survey when clients were babies/small children, as they are unlikely to condemn themselves during this period. This technique is usually employed when clients have begun to make progress on strengthening their adaptive belief in the present (Beck, 1995). In this example with Paul, the time period is during his teenage years (13–18 years):

Therapist: When we were assessing your problems at the beginning of therapy, you said that during adolescence (reading from the assessment form) 'that's when the pressure started to be successful at school, whatever'. Your brothers' achievements became the benchmarks for your own successes or failures.

Paul: That's right. I can remember that part of my life so well. I was always racing after my brothers to catch up, to be as good as them.

Therapist: That would reflect your 'I'm not good enough' belief. Could there be another way of looking at that period, or aspects of it, which could actually support the 'I'm good enough' belief'?

Paul: That's a tough one. I don't know how to see it differently.

Therapist: Presumably you want 'I'm good enough' to operate on your terms rather than on other people's.

Paul: Yes I do.

Therapist: So how would your teenage years look on your terms?

Paul: On my terms they were good.

Therapist: In what specific ways?

Paul: My school reports were generally good both academically and on the sports field. I had friends and a few girlfriends. Yes, I mean from that perspective I was good enough but it still doesn't feel right to say it.

Therapist: Because you're not yet convinced that you are good enough. Belief change takes time and doesn't happen overnight.

Padesky and Greenberger (1995, p. 150) state that 'it is not necessary to identify many experiences that support the new schema; even a few are meaningful to clients. Ideally, clients find one or two experiences per age period'.

The three schema change methods described in this section helped Paul gradually to weaken his adherence to his maladaptive beliefs and deepen his conviction in his new adaptive beliefs over the following weeks and months (the same change methods were used to strengthen his adaptive beliefs regarding others – 'People can be rejecting but also very supportive and kind').

The course of therapy

Paul spent a total of 15 sessions in therapy, with later ones being tapered-off: fortnightly, then monthly. During this period, Paul gradually assumed more responsibility for setting each session agenda, designing homework tasks, identifying problems and devising solutions to them; as Paul's level of activity in therapy increased, the therapist's (MN) decreased correspondingly and the therapist's role was reconceptualized as a consultant or mentor. Paul's depressed mood lifted, which was reflected in his self-reports and inventory scores:

- Beck Depression Inventory: 8 (normal range).
- Hopelessness Scale: 4 (mild hopelessness).

Paul's goals were achieved with the exception of finding another job (see Chapter 2). He thought this would be the acid test of his conviction in his new belief, but this belief incorporated successes and setbacks, not conclusive tests of personal worth; it quickly became apparent that Paul's old belief of 'I'm not good enough' and fear of potential rejection from others if he did not get a job or keep it was guiding his behaviour in this instance. This issue became part of relapse prevention, which is usually discussed in the last few sessions of CT: this approach identifies future situations (for example, adverse events, negative emotional states, inter-personal strife) that could trigger the return of clients' emotional problems and teaches them coping strategies to deal successfully with these situations (essentially, employing the tools and techniques of CT already learned). In Paul's case, he wrote down on a white card to remind himself that 'I'm good enough means accepting both successes and setbacks; it doesn't mean putting myself down whatever happens' whenever the old beliefs were triggered. We rehearsed this and other adaptive responses to his old negative thinking as preparation for terminating therapy.

Paul's sociotropically orientated personality often meant he sought the therapist's (MN) approval. It was pointed out to him this was the same trap he was setting himself in therapy that he habitually did outside. If approval was given continually this would reinforce his problems, not ameliorate them. Instead, we looked at developing greater self-acceptance rather than conditional self-acceptance based upon what others thought of him. Through this strategy, Paul was able to make the important distinction between wanting the approval and respect of others but no longer needing it (though this distinction blurred or temporarily disappeared when his dysfunctional beliefs were reactivated).

Follow-up appointments were negotiated to monitor and provide encouragement for Paul's progress as a self-therapist (sometimes called 'booster sessions'); if he encountered any difficulties he was unable to tackle himself, he could contact MN in advance of the appointment. His parting comment was: 'It's good to feel good enough'.

In this book so far, we have looked at CT from assessment to termination by following the case example of Paul. In the next and final chapter, we discuss some of the difficulties and obstacles that both clients and therapists experience during the course of therapy.

Chapter Six
Tackling Client and Therapist Difficulties in CT

In this final chapter, both client and therapist difficulties that arise in cognitive therapy are discussed and we look at ways to overcome them in order for clients to achieve their goals. Some of the client difficulties include an apparent inability to detect automatic thoughts, blaming situations for causing their emotional problems and not carrying out homework tasks; therapist difficulties include power struggles, counter-transference issues and failing to customize CT.

Client difficulties

Beck (1995, p. 300; Beck and Young, 1984; Persons, 1989) observes that 'problems of one kind or another arise with nearly every patient in cognitive therapy'. Therefore it is important for you to address them directly so these obstacles to client progress can be overcome.

'Nothing went through my mind when I was upset'

This comment or a variation of it is frequently heard in therapy as clients believe that their feelings have no cognitive antecedents or accompanying thoughts (for example, 'I wasn't thinking anything. I was quite happy and the next minute I'm bawling my eyes out'). As said in Chapter 1, NATs or images are involuntary, spontaneous and 'pop into' our minds often in times of emotional distress. We may know how we feel about a situation but not always what we think about it. Therefore, instead of trying to persuade clients that 'you are thinking something', it is important to train them to 'tune in' to these NATs by using, for example, any affect shift in therapy to demonstrate their presence (for example, 'When I mentioned some of the difficulties that might lie ahead in therapy, you sighed deeply.

What was going through your mind at that moment?' The client might reply in an angry tone: 'Why the hell can't anything ever be bloody easy for me?'). By sharpening their introspective skills, clients can learn to detect the automatic thoughts mediating their emotional reactions to events.

Confusing thoughts with feelings

Just because clients insert the word 'feel' into a sentence does not make it, in CT terms, a feeling (for example, 'I feel that my partner is drifting away from me'). This is an idea a client holds about her partner but, as yet, the therapist does not know how she *feels* about it. This is ascertained by asking the client directly: 'How do you feel about this thought that your partner is drifting away from you?' (Possible reply: 'Hurt'). Feelings can usually be summed up in one word (anger, depression, shame, guilt) whereas anything longer is a cognition. In order to reduce clients' confusion over the differences between thoughts and feelings, Beck et al. (1979, p. 37) advise that:

> it is desirable for the cognitive therapist to get an early start in making appropriate translations of 'I feel' into 'You believe. . .'.

These 'translations' are important in order to teach clients that thoughts and beliefs are hypotheses that can be tested and modified, whereas emotions are not subject to challenge.

'It's the situation, stupid!'

This was the retort of a client when the therapist (MN) was attempting to explain to her the CT view of emotional disturbance: namely, that it is our thoughts about events rather than the events themselves that lead to our emotional and behavioural reactions. When clients remain convinced that others or events dictate their emotional responses, little change can occur within the individual (for example, 'I'll feel better when my workload goes down'). Obviously, you will need to be non-dogmatically persistent and creative in demonstrating to your clients the CT viewpoint. For example, with the client who called the therapist 'stupid', an ABC analysis of the situation was carried out (see Chapter 2)

Table 6.1: ABC analysis of situation

A	B	C
Explaining the CT model	'You're talking crap! You're supposed to be helping me, not telling me it's all in my head.'	Anger

The client insisted that the therapist was making her angry, so she was asked what she would need to think about the same situation to feel less upset:

Table 6.2: ABC analysis continued

A	B	C
Explaining the CT model	'I suppose there could be something in what you're saying. It still sounds rather implausible though.'	Mildly irritable

Without diminishing in any way the adverse impact of unpleasant events, you can point out to your clients that by developing flexible thinking about their problems instead of insisting there is only one way to see them, they can establish greater emotional control and have more problem-solving options to consider.

With clients who insist that situations 'control' them, it might be helpful to use the example of Viktor Frankl, a famous psychiatrist, who endured the unspeakable horrors of Auschwitz and observed that 'everything can be taken from a man but one thing: the last of the human freedoms – to choose one's attitude in any given set of circumstances, to choose one's own way' (Frankl, 1985, p. 86). Whatever the circumstances, you can choose your attitude to events rather than have it dictated by the events.

Non-collaboration

Collaboration is a cornerstone of CT and 'requires an active stance on the part of both therapist and client to work together as a team' (Padesky and Greenberger, 1995, p. 6). Clients may enter therapy with preconceived ideas about what it entails ('I talk about my problems, you get into my head and sort them out, isn't that what you do?' or 'I sit here and you get me better'). These erroneous expectations of the client's role in therapy can be tackled by restructuring it:

Therapist: So you believe that if you just sit there and listen to me talking, then somehow you will get better. Is that right?

Client: Yeah, something like that.

Therapist: Okay. Now if, for example, you developed some back problems and your doctor told you the exercises you would need to do in order to strengthen your back, would your back automatically improve?

Client: No, not unless I did the actual exercises.

Therapist: Now with your psychological problems, if I show you ways of tackling them, will that be all that's needed to get better?

Client: Obviously not. I've got to do some work too.

Therapist: Can you see now why working together is important?

Client: I can now. You can only do so much for me, then I've got to do the rest. So what do I have to do then?

The therapist then explains in specific (but not exhaustive) detail what collaboration will actually require from each participant. Therapeutic collaboration forms part of clients' socialization into CT – if you leave discussing collaboration for several sessions clients are more likely to settle into the passive role and therefore more difficult to dislodge from it.

Not carrying out homework tasks

Homework provides opportunities for clients to put into practice the skills they have learned in the sessions and promotes faster and deeper progress. Not carrying out homework assignments or putting only minimal effort into them is one of the main areas of difficulty in CT. This may occur because clients do not understand what they are supposed to do and are too embarrassed to ask the therapist to explain it again, may lack the appropriate skills to execute the task or see the task as uninteresting or overwhelming.

Preparing the way for undertaking homework tasks can make their completion more likely. Therefore set homework collaboratively, not unilaterally, explain the rationale for assignments and their logical extension from the work done in the session, ascertain clients' level of skill and interest in them, undertake cognitive or behavioural rehearsal before practice *in vivo*, explain homework as an experiment to promote learning and not a success or failure endeavour, troubleshoot potential or actual obstacles to homework completion, gain feedback on homework-setting and ensure that you review homework in the next session. If some clients repeatedly do not carry out their assignments, you could, as a last resort, make the next appointment contingent upon them carrying out the homework task. As Walen, DiGiuseppe and Dryden (1992, p. 272) point out:

> Of course, the use of clinical judgment is necessary here; certainly this strategy would be contraindicated with a depressed patient or others whose problems require regular attention.

Transference reactions

Transference is the process 'whereby the client unconsciously relates to the counsellor/therapist as if to a significant person (or persons or aspects of persons) from the past' (Feltham and Dryden, 1993, p. 197). Transference reactions (lack of trust in authority figures, expecting to be rejected by the therapist) are treated in the same way as other automatic thoughts, that is identified, examined and adaptive responses formulated. Beck et al. (1990, p. 65) advise the therapist to 'look for tell-tale signs of a "transference" cognition. These are the same signs that suggest the presence of any automatic thoughts during the session ... one of the more revealing signs is a shift in the patient's gaze, especially if he or she has had a thought but prefers not to reveal it':

Therapist: It might be important for both of us to know what's in your mind at the present moment.

Client: Well, I think 'therapy is going to be a waste of time'.

Therapist: What leads you to believe it is going to be 'a waste of time'?

Client: My father thinks so. He just tells me to sort myself out. When I try to explain to him that I can't do it on my own, he just stares at the television or continues to read his newspaper.

Therapist: Do I remind you of that in some way?

Client: Well, you keep on writing things down as I'm talking to you. It's as if I haven't got your attention either. You probably think too 'he should be sorting himself out'.

Therapist: Well, I'm sorry if I've created that impression but I'm writing things down so I can remember what you've said. Would you like me to stop writing for a while and give you my full attention?

Client: That would be a start.

Therapist: Now you seem to believe you can read my mind, know what I'm thinking about. Is that true?

Client: No, I know I can't read your mind. So what are you thinking then?

Therapist: 'That if you could sort out your own problems, then you wouldn't be in therapy. As you are here, I want to do my best to help you.' That's what I'm thinking.

Client: How do I know if you mean it or not?

Therapist: What might be the answer to that?

Client: Stay in therapy for a while.

Therapist: Shall we give it three sessions, then come back to this issue?

Client: All right, I suppose it can't hurt.

By tackling transference reactions 'head on' (Beck et al., 1979) clients' distorted thinking can be addressed, thereby reducing some of the problems involved in constructing a collaborative relationship.

Feeling better versus getting better

Clients often leave therapy as soon as they feel better instead of staying on in order to get better. Burns (1980) describes feeling better as symptom-removal (answering NATs) whereas getting better is understanding and tackling those factors (underlying maladaptive beliefs) that predispose clients to experience their emotional problems (such as anxiety or depression) in the first place; if these beliefs are not modified and thereby left intact, this leaves clients vulnerable to future occurrences of their problems. Obviously you cannot prevent clients leaving therapy once symptom-removal is experienced, but providing a rationale for them to 'stay on' to work on schema-change means that 'more work now can produce fewer problems later'.

Involuntary clients

These are clients who do not come to therapy of their own volition (for example, those who are sent as part of a court order or 'given one last chance or else' by their employer or partner). The challenge with these clients is how to engage them constructively in therapy without this challenge degenerating into outright confrontation or coercion; if this occurs, any attempt at developing a collaborative relationship or encouraging clients to come back for further sessions will probably be destroyed:

Client: My wife thinks I've got an alcohol problem but I don't. She's threatening to leave me if I don't get help and that's the only reason I'm here and no other.

Therapist: Okay, fair enough. Presumably you want to save the relationship otherwise you wouldn't here (client nods). Given the fact that you are here though, how would you like to spend the time?

Client: My wife is always going on about my drinking – she doesn't drink – and therefore she doesn't know what she's talking about. One drink and she thinks you're a drunk. She's got the problem, not me.

[In order not to be seen as taking his wife's side, the therapist allows the client to ventilate his feelings about her for 20 minutes.]

Therapist: So from your perspective, she doesn't know the difference between moderate and heavy drinking?

Client: That's exactly right.

Therapist: Would you know the difference?

Client: Sure.

Therapist: What might be some of the signs that someone's drinking is slipping from moderate to heavy consumption?

[The therapist does not want to 'point an accusing finger' so she uses the anonymity of 'someone' to encourage the client to itemize some of the signs.]

Client: Well, I suppose down the pub every night, dinnertime, drinking before you go to work, time off work, lots of hangovers. That sort of thing.

Therapist: What about the inability to relax or enjoy oneself without a drink?

Client: Yeah, that too. I know some blokes like that.

Therapist: Do you think any of these things might apply to you?

Client: I don't think so. I like to drink in the evenings while watching television.

Therapist: Do you ever go to bed drunk?

Client: Sometimes. My wife doesn't like it of course.

Therapist: Why do you think you end up drunk?

Client: It's the only way to turn off.

Therapist: Turn off from what?

Client: I've got a lot of worries and pressures at work. I can't seem to turn off when I get home unless I have a drink.

Therapist: Shall we talk about some of these worries and pressures in the last half hour of the session?

Client: Can do if you want. Better than sitting here twiddling our thumbs I suppose.

[The client agreed eventually to a trial course of three sessions – 'It'll reassure my wife, if nothing else'.]

By not charging in at the outset of therapy and confronting the client with his 'denial', the therapist allows the client to put his side of the case ('She's got the problem, not me') before asking a series of probing questions that reveals the client's drinking pattern linked to pressures at work, which he agrees to explore over several sessions. In this way, an involuntary client becomes a voluntary one and the possibility of constructive problem-solving is glimpsed.

Rambling or garrulous clients

Obviously clients will want to talk about their problems and you need to hear what they have to say about them. However, some clients may talk about their problems at inordinate length or mentally wander from topic to topic (perhaps discussing their neighbours' problems, traffic jams, the state of the world). With these clients, your clinical focus may become blurred if not completely obscured by such behaviour. In order to regain your clinical focus, you can say something like the following to your clients: 'May I interrupt you there. I think I have enough initial information to understand your problems, so I would now like to show you a model or way of tackling them'.

Do not be afraid to interrupt politely your overly talkative clients: if you avoid doing this, therapy will probably get bogged down in verbiage and confusion with no clear goals to guide therapy. If you remain silent while the client 'verbally meanders, your silence may inaccurately convey to the client that he or she is making sense or doing constructive work' (Walen, DiGiuseppe and Dryden, 1992, p. 242).

All intellect but no feeling

These are clients who explain their problems in purely intellectual terms and claim they have no feelings about them. For example, 'My wife's infidelity is the logical outcome of a deteriorating relationship where intimacy is non-existent and two people have grown apart. I don't feel anything about the situation though'. You may hypothesize that the client is probably experiencing some painful affect and if this was activated in the session, some very hot cognitions would be revealed. Intellectualizing his problems guards against painful self-examination. Blackburn and Davidson (1995, p. 203) state that:

> if the patient cannot have access to his painful emotions, he and the therapist will not be able to elicit the negative thoughts which need attending to. Put simply, cognitive therapy cannot take place without first eliciting relevant emotional reactions.

Ways to elicit client affect include the appropriate use of humour, therapist modelling of emotional expression and employing imagery. Imagery, in particular, is a powerfully effective means of 'getting round' clients' defence mechanisms of intellectualization and rationalization (Young, 1994). Imagery provided the breakthrough with the above client, 'I wonder how you feel when you're sitting at home alone while imagining your wife spending the night with her boyfriend?' The client started to cry and said he felt deeply hurt and very angry. This provided the emotional 'way in' to allow a more accurate understanding of the client's presenting problems.

'I believe it intellectually but not emotionally'

This issue in therapy is often called the 'head–gut split'. The 'it' usually refers to a new and adaptive idea or belief that has some intellectual credibility for the client but not much, if any, emotional conviction for him. This distinction between intellectual and emotional insight is usually a problem of knowing something to be true but not believing it. Believing in a new idea is achieved by acting in support of it while acting against the old idea:

Client: I know up here (patting his head) that it's not the end of the world losing my job but I don't believe it down here (prodding his stomach).

Therapist: What blocks you from believing it in your gut?

Client: I'm not sure.

Therapist: How do you spend your time since you lost your job?

Client: Moping around the house, brooding on the unfairness of it all, that sort of thing.

Therapist: That sounds like you believe it is the end of the world rather than it isn't.

Client: Yeah, probably.

Therapist: In what ways would you need to behave if you wanted to believe it in your gut that losing your job wasn't the end of the world?

Client: Stop moping about, get off my backside and start looking for a job.

Therapist: Occasionally looking?

Client: No, every day if possible.

Therapist: And what might you notice if you start doing that?

Client: I'll be more motivated and more likely to get a job.

Therapist: And what will be going on down here? (prodding his stomach)

Client: That I'll believe it in my head as well as in my gut.

Therapist: So how do we start the march from the head to the gut?

Client: Go out tomorrow and start looking for a job. That can be the homework, right?

Therapist: Right.

Therapist difficulties

Therapists' difficulties in CT are conceptualized and dealt with in the same way as their clients' (in our experience as CT supervisors, we have noticed some therapists at a loss as to how they apply CT to themselves). It is important to remember that problems in therapy can emanate from you rather than always from your clients; so good CT supervision is essential to help you tackle these self-created difficulties.

'Your problems are all to do with your thinking'

This is what Gilbert (1992, p.147) calls 'the purely cognitive view, that we are in some sense socially decontextualised beings who disturb ourselves only by our thoughts'. This viewpoint is not, we would argue, standard CT, which views clients as contextualized beings whose life problems are not minimized. However, some therapists, particularly novice ones, may have a distorted view of CT and therefore communicate to clients that their problems 'are all in your head'. As well as possibly demeaning clients, it can also lead to blaming clients for their problems and is hardly the best way to build a therapeutic relationship, let alone a collaborative one. The point to get across to clients is that their maladaptive thinking about present problems can greatly exacerbate them, thereby creating the impression of hopelessness and helplessness in the face of them. By learning to modify such thinking and thereby ameliorating their emotional distress, clients can then focus on what steps to take to make changes in their social context (Clark, 1997).

Treating every thought as a NAT

This means not distinguishing between different types of cognitive data and therefore challenging every thought clients have about their problems or assuming that every thought is significant. This can lead to considerable confusion as key cognitions are not targeted:

Supervisor: Listening to your tape, you're challenging the client's thoughts 'I might not get the job. Some of the other candidates were better qualified than me'.

Therapist: That's what he's anxious about. Those are his negative thoughts, aren't they?

Supervisor: Well, couldn't it be true that he might not get the job or some of the other candidates were better qualified?

Therapist: I suppose so. I didn't think of that.

Supervisor: So in order really to understand the client's anxiety about these things, what will you need to tease out from him?

Therapist: What are the personal meanings or implications for him if he doesn't get the job or other candidates were better qualified than he was?

Supervisor: Exactly. You haven't got that yet. Maybe you want to write on a card 'Pursuing the personal meaning of events' to remind you of what?

Therapist: To remind me that's the pathway I need to follow if I want to find out what he's really anxious or upset about.

Supervisor: That will tell you what's going on up here (tapping head). That's the pathway you need to take for all clients.

By not pursuing the meanings clients attach to events, therapists will remain on the outside or outskirts of their clients' phenomenological world. Therefore clients' irrelevant, peripheral or less important cognitions will be targeted for examination and their key cognitions will be left undiscovered and unexamined, ready to inflict emotional harm when they are reactivated.

Being sucked into clients' viewpoints

Understanding a client's viewpoint is not the same as agreeing with it (for example, 'I can understand from what you've told me why you see yourself as undesirable but maybe there are other ways of interpreting the evidence that can help you to be less harsh on yourself'). When therapists become 'contaminated by the patient's thinking' (Fennell, 1989), they will struggle to help their clients develop different perspectives on their problems. As Beck et al. (1979, p. 59) point out:

> By stepping out of the role of the scientific observer, the therapist may 'buy into' the patient's distorted construction of reality. Instead of regarding the patient's negative interpretations as *hypotheses that require empirical testing,*

the therapist may begin to assume that these negative cognitions are accurate statements of fact which can be accepted at their face value [italics in original].

Therapist: The client says she is devastated by her husband leaving her and then she got made redundant. Talk about one problem after another. She's very depressed. I feel so sorry for her.

Supervisor: What are some of the key thoughts she has about these events in her life?

Therapist: (reading from the client's DTR) 'My life has been destroyed. I'll never be happy again.'

Supervisor: Have you managed to develop with her any initial alternative responses to these thoughts or tested them in some way?

Therapist: That's where I'm stuck. I keep thinking 'She's right to be depressed. Who wouldn't be depressed if these things happened to them?'

Supervisor: You sound as if you're letting the client's thinking influence your own. When you say 'Who wouldn't be depressed?' does that mean we would all be depressed in similar circumstances?

Therapist: Seems so.

Supervisor: Do you know others who haven't become depressed over bad events in their lives?

Therapist: (ponders) My father, a friend of mine.

Supervisor: Why do you think they didn't become depressed?

Therapist: My father is a strong character, and my friend never gets down no matter what happens to him.

Supervisor: Presumably they have certain beliefs that help them cope better with these situations.

Therapist: I would agree with that. My friend says 'Things could always be worse'.

Client: So is it true that we would all get depressed in similar circumstances?

Therapist: I guess not.

Supervisor: Because. . .?

Therapist: Because it depends on how you see the situation.

Supervisor: So is it possible to help your client develop a different and more constructive way of viewing her problems?

Therapist: Yes, but I've got to get my own thinking sorted out first.

Supervisor: Right. How will you do that?

Therapist: I'm not sure.

Supervisor: Well, we've already looked at one of your ideas about everyone being depressed if they experienced similar circumstances, but what about your other thought 'She's right to be depressed'?

Therapist: Well, I can say 'She's right if the evidence points that way after it has been tested and evaluated. If I agree with her before that's been done, I probably won't be able to help her'.

Supervisor: Good. We can evaluate how you are getting on at the next session.

'Buying into' clients' dysfunctional thinking is one example of countertransference, i.e. the thoughts and feelings the therapist has towards the client. Other examples might include getting angry because the client does not co-operate ('Why the hell does he bother coming if he's not prepared to work?') and feeling anxious about a client's imminent arrival ('I hope she doesn't attend because I've got no idea what to do with her'). In CT, 'countertransference issues are regarded as signals for therapists to work on their own automatic thoughts and assumptions' (Weishaar, 1993, p. 123).

Power struggles

These can occur if you believe you have to win arguments or disputes with your clients to prove, for example, 'I know best', 'I'm in charge', or 'I've been a therapist for ten years, so I know what I'm talking about. Now stop interrupting and just listen.' Power struggles involve winners and losers and valuable time and energy is wasted on trying to establish this pecking order in therapy. Arguing is a warning sign for you that a power struggle is emerging, a fight is about to begin. When this occurs:

> stop fighting. If you sense that the two of you are tugging at opposite ends of a rope, let go of your end. Try to go through an entire session without trying to convince the client of anything, and see what happens (Walen, DiGiuseppe and Dryden, 1992, p. 213).

Examine your own thoughts to see what is fuelling your needs for dominance or to convince the client of the correctness of your viewpoint or the CT model (these issues are often ego-related, for example 'If the client doesn't work hard in therapy, then he won't get better and I'll be seen as incompetent'). By developing adaptive responses ('If the client doesn't work hard in therapy, then he probably won't get better. This is his responsibility, not mine. My competence as a therapist does not depend upon his progress'), you can engage in constructive dialogue ('Of course, you can choose not to do any work in therapy, but I wonder where that will get you?') instead of power struggles.

Not socializing clients into CT

Some therapists may rush headlong into CT without adequately social-izing clients into this form of therapy; for example the importance of building a collaborative relationship, providing a rationale for under-taking homework, and the central focus on identifying and modifying negative thinking. Without explaining to clients their expected role in therapy, it is easy for clients to become confused or (understandably) resistant to the therapist's interventions. If clients have previous experi-ences of therapy, particularly more passive and non-directive approaches, CT may create a 'culture shock' when they are exposed to its active-direc-tive methods. Therefore, start socializing clients to the cognitive model of emotional disorders from the first session onwards. Additionally, and equally importantly, elicit feedback from clients throughout therapy to ascertain their level of understanding of, and agreement with, the cogni-tive model.

Failing to customize CT

It is self-evident that clients come to therapy from different social, cultural, economic, occupational and educational backgrounds. If therapy is presented as a 'one size fits all' approach instead of moulded to individual requirements, then some clients, perhaps many, will not benefit optimally from CT or terminate therapy prematurely. Such problems can be minimized by constructing a client profile, which then forms the basis for customizing therapy. For example, use language with which clients are familiar (avoid CT jargon whenever possible), monitor the pace of therapy (it may be too fast or too slow), find out what was helpful or unhelpful about previous experiences of therapy ('The therapist never said much, which I didn't like'), ascertain the kind of relationship clients prefer to have with the therapist (as long as it does not reinforce their existing problems), explore previous problem-solving experiences ('If things are kept simple, then I know what I've got to do'). By customizing CT in this way, clients are more likely to engage collaboratively in therapy rather than feel it has been imposed on them.

Summary

In this book, we hope we have provided you with the essential elements of cognitive therapy. Let us remind you of some of what we have done.

In Chapter 1, we discussed CT's basis as an information-processing model in understanding emotional disorders, the structural organization of thinking that links surface cognitions (negative automatic thoughts or NATs) to core beliefs (schemas) and the reciprocal relationship between thoughts, feelings, behaviours, physiology and environment in assessing clients' problems.

In Chapter 2, we showed you how to develop a case conceptualization approach (assessment), which consisted of three elements:

- a detailed description of the presenting problem
- an ABC cross-sectional analysis of it
- the historical context of the present problem, which included identifying longstanding underlying assumptions and core beliefs.

Running alongside the assessment, we described the process of socializing clients into CT.

In Chapter 3, we looked at ways of eliciting NATs through the use of techniques such as guided discovery and in-session affect shifts; the importance of distinguishing thoughts from feelings; and helping clients' to reality-test their NATs through methods such as behavioural experiments, decatastrophizing and re-attribution.

In Chapter 4, we emphasized the central importance of homework as clients apply the CT skills learned in therapy to their everyday lives. This enables them to weaken support for their maladaptive thinking and strengthen their conviction in their new and adaptive ideas.

In Chapter 5, we focused on ways of identifying underlying beliefs (conditional assumptions, rules and core beliefs) through techniques such as the downward arrow, pinpointing 'shoulds' and 'musts', and discerning themes in clients' NATs. Examining assumptions and rules included looking at their historical development, use of imagery and listing their advantages and disadvantages; with schema or core belief change we demonstrated three key techniques: the use of a continuum, positive data logs and historical tests.

Finally, in this chapter, we discussed some of the difficulties and obstacles encountered by clients and therapists alike, and ways to overcome them so that clients' goals for change can be realized.

In conclusion, cognitive therapy provides a time limited, structured and present-orientated approach to emotional and behavioural problem-solving. Since its development in the early 1960s, cognitive therapy 'has become the single most important and best validated psychotherapeutic approach. It is the psychological treatment of choice for a wide range of psychological problems' (Salkovskis, 1996, p. xiii). CT's potential for further development and application seems limitless.

Appendix

For information on training in the United Kingdom in CT contact:

Howard Lomas
British Association for Behavioural and Cognitive Psychotherapies
PO Box 9
Accrington BB5 2GD
UK
Tel: (44) 01254 875277

For details on CT training worldwide contact:

International Association for Cognitive Psychotherapy
Beck Institute for Cognitive Therapy
GSB Building, Suite 700
City Line and Belmont Avenues
Bala Cynwyd
PA 19004-1610
USA

Tel: (001) 610/664-3020

References

American Psychiatric Association (1994). Diagnostic and Statistical Manual of Mental Disorders (fourth edition). Washington, DC: American Psychiatric Association.

Barlow, D.H. and Craske, M.G. (1989). Mastery of your Anxiety and Panic. Albany, NY: Graywind Publications.

Beck, A.T. (1972). Depression: Causes and Treatment. Philadelphia, PA: University of Pennsylvania Press.

Beck, A.T. (1976). Cognitive Therapy and the Emotional Disorders. New York: International Universities Press.

Beck, A.T. (1987). Cognitive models of depression. Journal of Cognitive Psychotherapy, 1 (1), 5–37.

Beck, A.T. (1988). Love is Never Enough. New York: Harper & Row.

Beck, A.T. (1996). Beyond belief: a theory of modes, personality and psychopathology. In: P.M. Salkovskis (Ed.), Frontiers of Cognitive Therapy. New York: Guilford Press.

Beck, A.T., Brown, G., Steer, R.A., Eidelson, J.I. and Riskind, J.H. (1987). Differentiating anxiety and depression: a test of the cognitive content-specificity hypothesis. Journal of Abnormal Psychology, 96, 179–183.

Beck, A.T. and Emery, G. (1979) Cognitive Therapy of Anxiety and Phobic Disorders. Philadelphia, PA: Center for Cognitive Therapy.

Beck, A.T., Emery, G. and Greenberg, R.L. (1985). Anxiety Disorders and Phobias: A Cognitive Perspective. New York: Basic Books.

Beck, A.T., Epstein, N., Brown, G. and Steer, R.A. (1988). An inventory for measuring clinical anxiety: psychometric properties. Journal of Consulting and Clinical Psychology, 56, 893–897.

Beck, A.T., Freeman, A. and Associates (1990). Cognitive Therapy of Personality Disorders. New York: Guilford.

Beck, A.T., Rush, A.J., Shaw, B.F. and Emery, G. (1979). Cognitive Therapy of Depression. New York: Guilford.

Beck, A.T., Ward, C.H., Mendelson, M., Mock, J. and Erbaugh, J. (1961). An inventory for measuring depression. Archives of General Psychiatry, 4, 561–571.

Beck, A.T. and Weishaar, M.E. (1989). Cognitive therapy. In: R.J. Corsini and D Wedding (eds), Current Psychotherapies. Itasca, IL: F.E. Peacock Publishers.

Beck, A.T., Weissman, A., Lester, D. and Trexler, L. (1974). The measurement of pessimism: the hopelessness scale. Journal of Consulting and Clinical Psychology, 42, 861–865.

Beck, A.T., Wright, F.D., Newman, C.F. and Liese, B.S. (1993). Cognitive Therapy of Substance Abuse. New York: Guilford.

Beck, A.T. and Young, J.E. (1984). Cognitive therapy of depression. In: D. Barlow (Ed.), Clinical Handbook of Psychological Disorders: A Step-By-Step Treatment Manual. New York: Guilford Press.

Beck, J.S. (1995). Cognitive Therapy: Basics and Beyond. New York: Guilford.

Blackburn, I.M. and Davidson, K. (1995). Cognitive Therapy for Depression and Anxiety, amended. Oxford: Oxford Scientific Publications.

Blackburn, I.M. and Twaddle, V. (1996). Cognitive Therapy in Action. London: Souvenir Press.

Blackburn, I.M. (1996). A case of depression. In: I.M. Blackburn and V. Twaddle, Cognitive Therapy in Action. London: Souvenir Press.

Bond, F.W. (1998). Using a case formulation to understand and treat a person with generalised anxiety disorder. In: M. Bruch and F.W. Bond (eds), Beyond Diagnosis: Case Formulation Approaches in CT. Chichester: John Wiley & Sons.

Bruch, M. (1998). The development of case formulation approaches. In: M. Bruch & F.W. Bond (eds), Beyond Diagnosis: Case Formulation Approaches in CT. Chichester: John Wiley & Sons.

Burns, D.D. (1980). Feeling Good: The New Mood Therapy. New York: William Morrow.

Burns, D.D. (1989). The Feeling Good Handbook. New York: William Morrow.

Burns, D.D. and Auerbach, A.H. (1992). Does homework compliance enhance recovery from depression? Psychiatric Annals, 22, 464–469.

Burns, D.D. and Nolen-Hoeksema, S. (1991). Coping styles, homework compliance, and the effectiveness of cognitive-behavioral therapy. Journal of Consulting and Clinical Psychology, 59, 305–311.

Butler, G. and Hope, T. (1995). Manage your Mind. Oxford: Oxford University Press.

Clark, D.A. (1995). Perceived limitations of standard cognitive therapy: a consideration of efforts to revise Beck's theory and therapy. Journal of Cognitive Psychotherapy, 9 (3), 153–172.

Clark, D.A. (1997). Is cognitive therapy ill-founded? A commentary on Lyddon and Weill. Journal of Cognitive Psychotherapy, 11 (2), 91–98.

Clark, D.A., Beck, A.T. and Brown, G. (1989). Cognitive mediation in general psychiatric outpatients: a test of the content-specificity hypothesis. Journal of Personality and Social Psychology, 56, 958–964.

Clark, D.A. and Steer, R.A. (1996). Empirical status of the cognitive model of anxiety and depression. In: P.M. Salkovskis (Ed.), Frontiers of Cognitive Therapy. New York: Guilford.

Clark, D.M. (1986). A cognitive approach to panic. Behaviour Research and Therapy, 24, 461–470.

Clark, D.M. (1988). A cognitive model of panic. In: S. Rachman and J. Maser, (eds), Panic: Psychological Perspectives. Hillsdale, NJ: Lawrence Erlbaum.

Clark, D.M. (1989). Anxiety states. In: K. Hawton, P.M. Salkovskis, J. Kirk and D.M. Clark (eds), Cognitive Therapy for Psychiatric Problems. Oxford: Oxford University Press.

Clark, D.M. and Fairburn, C.G. (eds) (1997). Science and Practice of Cognitive therapy. Oxford: Oxford University Press.

Dattilio, F.M. and Freeman, A. (1992). Introduction to cognitive therapy. In: A. Freeman and F.M. Dattilio (eds), Comprehensive Casebook of Cognitive Therapy. New York: Plenum.

Dattilio, F.M. and Padesky, C.A. (1990). Cognitive Therapy with Couples. Sarasota, FL: Professional Resource Exchange.

DiGiuseppe, R. (1991a). A rational–emotive model of assessment. In: M.E. Bernard (Ed.), Using Rational–Emotive Therapy Effectively: A Practitioner's Guide. New York: Plenum.

DiGiuseppe, R. (1991b). Comprehensive cognitive disputing in RET. In: M.E. Bernard (Ed.), Using Rational–Emotive Therapy Effectively: A Practitioner's Guide. New York: Plenum.

Ellis, A. (1994). Reason and Emotion in Psychotherapy, revised and updated. Secaucus, NJ: Carol Publishing Group.

Ellis, A. and MacLaren, C. (1998). Rational Emotive Behavior Therapy: A Therapist's Guide. San Luis Obispo, CA: Impact Publishers.

Fairburn, C.G. and Cooper, P.J. (1989). Eating disorders. In: K. Hawton, P.M. Salkovskis, J. Kirk and D.M. Clark (eds), Cognitive therapy for Psychiatric Problems. Oxford: Oxford University Press.

Feltham, C. and Dryden, W. (1993). Dictionary of Counselling. London: Whurr.

Fennell, M.J.V. (1989). Depression. In: K. Hawton, P.M. Salkovskis, J. Kirk and D.M. Clark (eds), Cognitive therapy for Psychiatric Problems. Oxford: Oxford University Press.

Fennell, M.J.V. (1997). Low self-esteem: a cognitive perspective. Behavioural and Cognitive Psychotherapy, 25 (1), 1–25.

Freeman, A. (1992). The development of treatment conceptualizations in cognitive therapy. In: A. Freeman and F.M. Dattilio (eds), Comprehensive Casebook of Cognitive Therapy. New York: Plenum Press.

Frankl, V. E. (1985). Man's Search for Meaning. New York: Washington Square Press. (Originally published in German in 1946.)

Gilbert, P. (1992). Counselling for Depression. London: Sage Publications.

Gilbert, P. (1997). Overcoming Depression. London: Robinson.

Gilbert, P. (1998). Shame and humiliation in the treatment of complex cases. In: N. Tarrier, A. Wells and G. Haddock (eds), Treating Complex Cases: The Cognitive Behavioural Therapy Approach. Chichester: John Wiley & Sons.

Greenberger, D. and Padesky, C.A. (1995). Mind Over Mood: A Cognitive Therapy Treatment Manual for Clients. New York: Guilford.

Hauck, P. (1982). How To Do What You Want To Do. London: Sheldon Press.

Herbert, C. and Wetmore, A. (1999). Overcoming Traumatic Stress. London: Robinson.

Kennerley, H. (1997). Overcoming Anxiety. London: Robinson.

Kroese, B.S., Dagnan, D. and Loumidis, K. (eds) (1997). Cognitive-Behaviour Therapy for People with Learning Disabilities. London: Routledge.

Mahoney, M. and Lyddon, W. (1988). Recent developments in cognitive approaches to counseling and psychotherapy. Counseling Psychology, 16, 190–234.

Maultsby, M.C. (1971). Systematic written homework in psychotherapy. Psychotherapy: Theory, Research, and Practice, 8, 195–198.

Moorey, S. (1990). Cognitive therapy. In: W. Dryden (Ed.), Individual Therapy: A Handbook. Buckingham: Open University Press.

Neenan, M. and Dryden, W. (2000). The Essential Rational Emotive Behaviour Therapy. London: Whurr.

Neenan, M. and Palmer, S. (1998). A cognitive-behavioural approach to tackling stress. Counselling, the Journal of the British Association for Counselling, 9 (4), 315–319.

Neimeyer, R. and Feixas, G. (1990). The role of homework and skill acquisition in the outcome of group cognitive therapy for depression. Behavior Therapy, 21, 282–292.

Nelson-Jones, R. (1995). The Theory and Practice of Counselling (second edition). London: Cassell.

Nelson-Jones, R. (1998). Using the whiteboard in lifeskills counselling. The Rational Emotive Behaviour Therapist, the Journal of the Association for Rational Emotive Behaviour Therapists, 6 (2), 77–88.

Padesky, C.A. (1993a). Socratic questioning: changing minds or guiding discovery? Keynote address to European Congress of Behavioural and Cognitive Therapies, London.

Padesky, C.A. (1993b). Schema as self-prejudice. International Cognitive Therapy Newsletter, 5/6, 16–17.

Padesky, C.A. (1994). Schema change processes in cognitive therapy. Clinical Psychology and Psychotherapy, 1 (5), 267–278.

Padesky, C.A. and Greenberger, D. (1995). Clinician's Guide to Mind Over Mood. New York: Guilford.

Perris, C. (1989). Cognitive Therapy with Schizophrenic Patients. New York: Guilford.

Persons, J.B. (1989). Cognitive Therapy in Practice: A Case Formulation Approach. New York: W.W. Norton.

Persons, J.B., Burns, D.D. and Perloff, J.M. (1988). Predictors of drop-out and outcome in cognitive therapy for depression in a private practice setting. Cognitive Therapy and Research, 12, 557–575.

Reinecke, M.A. (1994). Suicide and depression. In: F.M. Dattilio and A. Freeman (eds), Cognitive–Behavioral Strategies in Crisis Intervention. New York: Guilford Press.

Reinecke, M.A., Dattilio, F.M. and Freeman, A. (eds) (1996). Cognitive Therapy with Children and Adolescents. New York: Guilford.

Richman, D.R. (Ed.) (1992). Cognitive therapy at work. Journal of Cognitive Psychotherapy, 6 (4), 227–304.

Rogers, C.R. (1957). The necessary and sufficient conditions of therapeutic personality change. Journal of Consulting Psychology, 12, 95–103.

Salkovskis, P.M. (1991). The importance of behaviour in the maintenance of anxiety and panic: a cognitive account. Behavioural Psychotherapy, 19, 6–19.

Salkovskis, P.M. (1996). Preface. In: P.M. Salkovskis (Ed.), Frontiers of Cognitive Therapy. New York: Guilford.

Salkovskis, P.M. (1996). Cognitive therapy and Aaron T. Beck. In: P.M. Salkovskis (Ed.), Frontiers of Cognitive Therapy. New York: Guilford.

Salkovskis, P.M. and Kirk, J. (1989). Obsessional disorders. In: K. Hawton, P.M. Salkovskis, J. Kirk and D.M. Kirk (eds), Cognitive therapy for Psychiatric Problems. Oxford: Oxford University Press.

Scott, M.J., Stradling, S.G. and Dryden, W. (1995). Developing Cognitive–Behavioural Counselling. London: Sage Publications.

Tinch, C.S. and Friedberg, R.D. (1996). The schema identification worksheet: a guide for clients and clinicians. International Cognitive Therapy Newsletter, 10 (4), 1–4.

Vallis, T.M., Howes, J.L. and Miller, P.C. (eds) (1991). The Challenge of Cognitive Therapy. New York: Plenum.

Walen, S.R., DiGiuseppe, R. and Dryden, W. (1992). A Practitioner's Guide to Rational–Emotive Therapy. New York: Oxford University Press.

Weishaar, M.E. (1993). Aaron T. Beck. London: Sage Publications.

Weishaar, M.E. (1996) Developments in Cognitive Therapy: 1960–95. In: W. Dryden (Ed.), Developments in Psychotherapy: Historical Perspectives. London: Sage Publications.

Weishaar, M.E. and Beck, A.T. (1986). Cognitive therapy. In: W. Dryden and W. Golden (eds), Cognitive–Behavioural Approaches to Psychotherapy. London: Harper & Row.

Weissman, A.N. and Beck, A.T. (1978). Development and validation of the dysfunctional attitude scale. Paper presented at the Annual Meeting of the American Educational Research Association, Toronto, Canada.

Wells, A. (1997). Cognitive Therapy of Anxiety Disorders. Chichester: John Wiley & Sons.

Wills, F. and Sanders, D. (1997). Cognitive Therapy: Transforming the Image. London: Sage Publications.

Wright J.H., Thase, M., Beck, A T. and Ludgate, J.W. (eds) (1993). Cognitive Therapy with Inpatients: Developing a Cognitive Milieu. New York: Guilford.

Young, J. E. (1994). Cognitive Therapy for Personality Disorders: A Schema-Focused Approach (revised edition). Sarasota, FL: Professional Resource Press.

Young, J. and Behary, W.T. (1998). Schema-focused therapy for personality disorders. In: N. Tarrier, A. Wells and G. Haddock (eds), Treating Complex Cases: The Cognitive Behavioural Therapy Approach. Chichester: John Wiley & Sons.

Young, J.E. and Lindemann, M.D. (1992). An integrative schema-focused model for personality disorders. Journal of Cognitive Psychotherapy, 6 (1), 11–23.

Index